# FACTS AT YOUR FINGERTIPS

# INVENTION AND TECHNOLOGY
# MEDICINE AND HEALTH

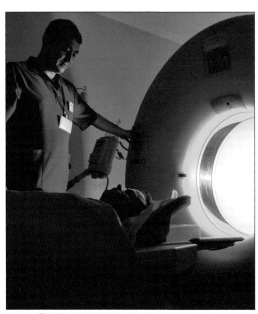

BROWN
BEAR
BOOKS

**Published by Brown Bear Books Ltd**

4877 N. Circulo Bujia
Tucson, AZ 85718
USA

**and**

First Floor
9-17 St. Albans Place
London N1 0NX

© 2012 Brown Bear Books Ltd

Library of Congress Cataloging-in-Publication Data

Medicine and health / edited by Tom Jackson.
    p. cm.
Audience: 9-12.
Summary: "Describes the evolution of medical technology and what doctors know about human health issues, including anatomy, surgery, drugs, and reproduction. A timeline traces the progress of ancient medical practices and beliefs to modern technology"– Provided by publisher.
Includes index.
    ISBN 978-1-936333-38-7 (library binding)
1. Medicine–History. 2. Medicine, Preventive–History. I. Jackson, Tom, 1972-

RA424.M43 2012
610–dc23

2012004786

**Editorial Director:** Lindsey Lowe
**Editor:** Tom Jackson
**Creative Director:** Jeni Child
**Designer:** Lynne Lennon
**Children's Publisher:** Anne O'Daly
**Production Director:** Alastair Gourlay

Printed in the United States of America

Picture Credits

**Front Cover:** Shutterstock, Mark Herreid
**Back Cover:** Konuk Levent

**Corbis:** Salvatore De Nolfi 49t; **Getty Images:** Hulton Archive 29bk 51; SSPL 16t **Public Domain:** 5b; Alokprasad 41t; NLM 8t **Shutterstock:** 28; Konuk Levent 1; Denis Kornilv 4bl; Andrey Kiselev Valerevich 30b; Martin Valigursky 52b; Dusan Zidar 24 **Thinkstock:** Brand X Pictures 54t; Comstock 3, 22tr, 33tr, 48, 49b, 50t; Digital Vision 29t; Hemera 6t. 52t, 56; Istockphoto 8b 12t, 14, 18b, 19br, 23tr, 32, 35br, 42, 59t 60b; Photodisc 20b, 30, 38; PhotoObjecs.net 35t; Photos.com 4-5, 6b, 7t, 10t, 13b. 15t, 16b, 17b, 18t, 19bl. 20t, 22bl, 23bl, 27t, 36, 41b, 50b, 60l; Polka Dot 34t;  Stockbyte 30t, 33b, 34b,  40, 54b, 58, 61t **Topfoto:** 26t; World History Archive 11t, 15b

*Brown Bear Books has made every attempt to contact the copyright holder. If you have any information please email smortimer@windmillbooks.co.uk*

All artwork copyright Brown Bear Books Ltd

# CONTENTS

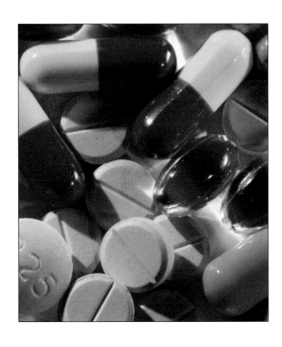

Medicine as we know it today is a well-developed and sophisticated area of science. But its humble beginnings can be traced back thousands of years to prehistoric society.

**Most prehistoric peoples** lived in small groups and wandered from place to place, using materials such as bone, wood, and stone to construct simple tools. The study of their skeletons reveals that they could reset broken bones and perform minor operations with a

## SUPERNATURAL CURES

It was not only prehistoric peoples who thought diseases could be caused by magic and spirits. The ancient Egyptians, whose civilization began around 3000 B.C., were also firm believers in the supernatural. They often wore charms to keep evil spirits away, and if they did become ill, they usually turned to magic and their gods to cure them. The ancient Greeks and Romans constructed temples to Asclepius, the god of healing, to which the sick were often brought to receive miracle cures. Throughout the Middle Ages, when Christianity had become the main religion in Europe, sick people often went on pilgrimages to holy sites, hoping for relief. Even today supernatural cures and witch doctors—who often practice herbal medicine—are important in many parts of the world.

◄ *Asclepius, the Greek god of healing, had a staff entwined with a snake. This symbol is used by medical institutions to this day.*

▲ *All illness was potentially deadly before modern medicines were invented, but calling for a doctor was expensive and so was often a last resort.*

reasonable success rate. However, when an illness was more serious, they probably believed that the sufferer was possessed by an evil spirit.

Prehistoric people performed one major operation: trepanning, or cutting a hole in the skull of a person while they were still alive. Trepanned skulls have been found in every part of the world. Many of the skulls have new bone growth around the edges of the hole, showing that the person probably lived on for many years after the operation.

### Herbal remedies

Ancient cures were often a combination of herbal and magical elements. Chest conditions were treated by making the patient inhale steam, while cuts and burns were treated with ointments. Often the doctor would read incantations or perform ceremonies as the treatment was administered. Egyptian records show that if a treatment worked, people continued to use it, while those treatments that failed were soon forgotten. In this way, the ancient Egyptians built up a lot of medical knowledge, and many of their treatments are still used in some parts of the world.

## THE BOOKS OF THOTH

The most important early Egyptian medical books were the *Books of Thoth*, kept by priests at the temple to Thoth, the Egyptian god of wisdom. Although none of these works has survived, researchers have found a medical book from around 1500 B.C. that was probably based on them. It contains detailed instructions on how to deal with many common illnesses.

From the periods of Greek and Roman civilization to the end of the 18th century, herbal cures were very widely used. New herbal treatments were always being added to the growing body of medical knowledge. There was little science involved in this area of medicine, and no one knew why the treatments worked. For example, it has been known for hundreds of years that the bark of certain trees cures

▼ *A prehistoric human skull has a hole in it from a trepanning procedure.*

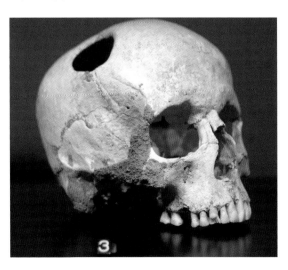

headaches when chewed. However, it was only in the 19th century that the substance responsible for this effect, salicylic acid (now used to make aspirin), was isolated. Another century passed before its method of action was discovered. Today an increasing number of people are reverting to these tried and tested herbal remedies because they are worried about possible side effects of modern drugs.

*◄ Hippocrates, the founder of modern medicine, rejected the idea that diseases had a supernatural cause—and that magic was an important part of treatment.*

## Theories of disease

The ancient Egyptians were the first people to devise a theory of disease, allowing them to develop treatments for serious illnesses in a systematic manner. Influenced by the seasonal rise and fall of the Nile River, which was very important to Egyptian people, doctors thought that the human body must be full of channels for blood and other fluids. The blockage of one of these channels would lead to illness, and treatments such as emetics (substances that cause vomiting), laxatives, and bleeding (drawing out blood) were widely used to clear blockages and cure the patient.

One of the greatest individual contributors to medical knowledge

---

## CLINICAL OBSERVATION AND DIAGNOSIS

Hippocrates set out the principles of diagnosis. He observed symptoms to predict the course of the disease. Once a prognosis (prediction) had been made, he administered treatment while monitoring the patient. Modern doctors still use this approach, known as clinical observation.

Later doctors invented tests that made the diagnosis more precise. Temperature can be used to gauge illness, for example. In 1626 an Italian physician called Santorio (1561-1636) invented a water thermometer that allowed doctors to measure temperature with greater accuracy. Medieval doctors listened to a patient's lungs and heart. A technique called percussion was developed by Austrian Leopold Auenbrügger (1722-1809). He tapped a patient's abdomen to listen to other internal organs as well.

The microscope was first used to study disease by Athanasius Kircher (1602-1680) in the late 1600s, but its true medical potential did not become apparent for another century.

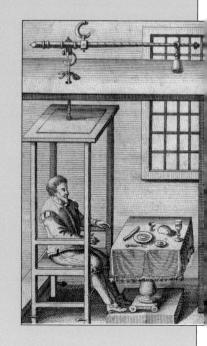

*▶ Santorio used a simple weighing experiment to show that the body extracted substances from food before expelling waste material.*

▲ *During Europe's Black Death epidemics, plague victims were collected each night for immediate burial, lest the then-mysterious disease spread to the living.*

was a Greek physician called Hippocrates, who lived from around 460 B.C. to 377 B.C. We know very little about Hippocrates himself, but he is associated with a collection of medical texts written around 430 B.C. Hippocrates devised his own theory of disease. He thought that the body was made up of four humors—blood, phlegm, black bile, and yellow bile. He suggested that in a healthy body the humors are all finely balanced, but if this balance is disrupted, illness results. His theory of disease was widely used by European doctors, throughout the Middle Ages.

### Anatomy

The ancient Egyptians made several advances in anatomy—the study of the structure of the body—while learning how to preserve, or mummify, dead bodies, which they believed were still needed in the afterlife.

## HEALTH AND LIFESTYLE

The connection between cleanliness and health was probably first made by the ancient Egyptians, who washed both their clothes and their bodies regularly. Toilets and baths were common among the rich, and some Egyptians even slept under mosquito nets! Like the Egyptians, the Greeks and Romans knew of the benefits of a healthy lifestyle. Greek physician Diocles, who lived in the 4th century B.C., advocated washing with pure water every day and even cleaning the teeth with peppermint-flavored powder. The Romans turned bathing into a social event, building great public baths in many of their cities.

With the fall of the Roman Empire sewers and aqueducts (channels that carried fresh water into towns and cities) fell into disrepair, and living standards declined. Filthy streets and poor food and water hygiene led to outbreaks of plague and other infectious diseases during the Middle Ages. It was not until the Industrial Revolution during the 19th century that conditions began to improve.

▼ *A public bath was a central part of a Roman city. Bathers plunged into pools of different temperatures, and used olive oil to clean the skin. Soap had yet to be invented.*

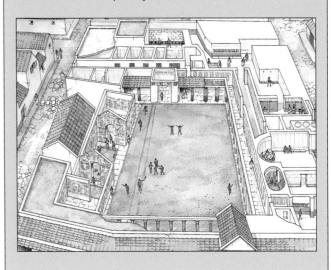

*◀ The work of Galen, a doctor during the Roman period, influenced doctors until the 17th century.*

Galen, a physician working in Rome in the 2nd century A.D., dissected humans and monkeys to study anatomy. Although many of his findings were incorrect, Galen's picture of the human body remained unchallenged for centuries.

Flemish anatomist Andreas Vesalius (1514–1564) was the first to improve on Galen's theory of anatomy. He drew detailed pictures of body systems, building up layer upon layer of anatomical features in the body. Vesalius's book *On the Fabric of the Human Body* (1543) corrected several of Galen's mistakes, but did not challenge Galen's view of blood movement. In 1559 Italian anatomist Realdo Colombo (1516–1559) showed that blood passed from one side of the heart to the other via the lungs. This finding led English physician and anatomist William Harvey (1578–1657) to show how blood circulated through the body. Tiny blood vessels, called capillaries, that ran through all body parts were discovered later by Italian anatomist Marcello Malpighi (1628–1694).

## SOCIETY AND INVENTIONS

### Hospitals and medical schools

The Romans needed healthy soldiers to sustain their empire, and developed the first system of public health. State doctors were appointed to tend to the poor, and hospitals were built in many cities. Following the collapse of the Roman world in the 5th century A.D., however, doctors were in short supply. The poor had to make do with herbal remedies and barbers set bones, pulled teeth (right), and stitched wounds. The first medical school was set up around A.D. 1100 at Salerno in Italy. Soon similar schools were established all over Europe. Doctors and hospitals were, however, still too expensive for most people—and only located in major cities. Widespread, affordable health care did not become available until the 20th century.

## The circulation of the blood

William Harvey discovered how blood moved around the body in the early 17th century. His findings contradicted the theory proposed by Galen that had been taught to doctors for centuries. Galen thought that blood was made inside the heart and liver and drawn into the body where it was used up—soon replaced by new blood. Harvey's experiments showed that if this were true a person would be making 550 lb (250 kg) of blood a day! Perhaps inspired by the steam-driven pumps that were coming into use around the same time, Harvey saw that the heart was a four-chambered pump. As blood passes through the body, the oxygen that it carries is used up. This blood, called deoxygenated blood (shown in blue), then enters the right atrium (chamber) of the heart. From there it is pumped into the right ventricle and then to the lungs, where it absorbs more oxygen. Oxygen-carrying blood (red) then passes back to the heart, entering the left atrium and flowing into the left ventricle, the most powerful chamber, which pumps the blood back to the tissues of the body. Vessels that carry blood toward the heart are called veins, while those that carry blood away from the heart are arteries. Valves inside both the veins and the heart itself stop blood from flowing in the wrong direction.

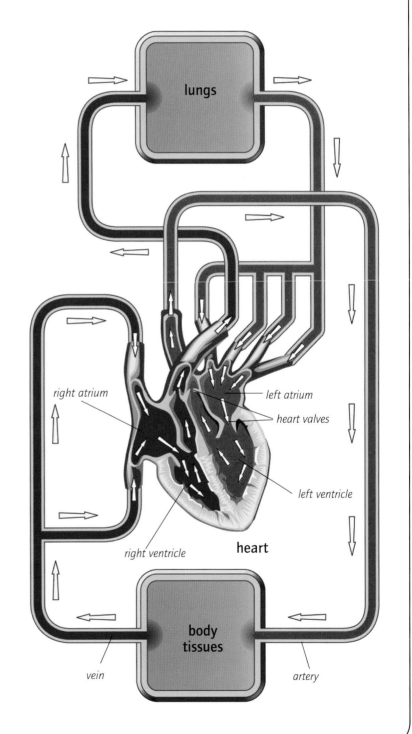

▲ *Early surgery, such as a leg amputation, was fast and brutal. It had to be because the patient was still awake.*

## Surgery

Egyptian surgeons probably performed minor operations, such as the removal of cysts and lumps. Most were successful because wounds were treated with the leaves and bark of willow, which contains a natural antiseptic to kill germs. Surgery was hazardous in ancient Greece because human dissection was banned, and surgeons had very little knowledge of human anatomy. The work of Galen led to improvements, but much of this knowledge was lost with the fall of the Roman Empire around A.D. 500.

Surgery was considered manual work in medieval Europe, and most doctors refused to perform it. Instead, operations were left to barbers, who mostly cut hair.

## FACTS AND FIGURES

**Plague** This name can refer to any epidemic (widespread outbreak of disease) that claims many lives. A major outbreak of plague occurred in Europe around A.D. 542. Another outbreak, between 1346 and 1353, claimed 25 million lives—almost a quarter of the total population. Medieval doctors had no way of treating plague, and many lost their own lives to the disease.

**Leprosy** One of the oldest known diseases, an Egyptian skeleton from around 500 B.C. shows signs of the disease. With no effective treatments available, millions of people died from leprosy during the Middle Ages. Today the disease is still present in many parts of the world, and it is estimated that 10 million people suffer from it.

**Syphilis** Syphilis had been identified in 4,000-year-old skeletons from central Russia, but the first European outbreak occurred in 1493. Sailors on Christopher Columbus's voyage may have carried the disease to Europe from the Americas. Medieval treatments involving herbal remedies and mercury were not effective, and the disease developed for many years before becoming fatal.

The two main problems with surgery are pain and infection: medieval surgeons tried to tackle both. Italian surgeon Hugh of Lucca bathed wounds in wine to prevent infection, but the idea was not generally adopted. Attempts were made to dull pain by drugging patients before operations, but this practice also seems to have died out.

Ambroise Paré (1510–1590), a French surgeon, wrote several books that improved the standard of medieval surgery. He stressed the importance of avoiding excessive pain, advocating quick and simple operations, and condemning the use of cruel techniques such as burning wounds to stop them bleeding.

Despite these advances, surgery continued to be dangerous until medicine became more scientific during the 19th century, around the time of the Industrial Revolution.

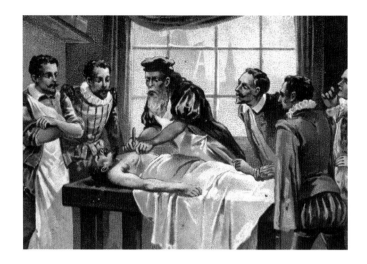

▶ *Ambroise Paré was a 16th-century French surgeon. He rediscovered a Roman ointment made from egg white and turpentine to stop incisions from becoming infected.*

## KEY COMPONENTS

### Ancient Egyptian surgeon's bag

This relief is carved into the wall of the more than 2,000-year-old Egyptian temple at Kom Ombo. The collection is located close to other reliefs showing medical scenes, such as the queen giving birth, and some scholars believe it shows a selection of surgical tools. There are no written descriptions of the instruments, and the uses of some are not known. Some of the tools that have been identified are listed below.

**1** Knives probably used to make incisions (cuts) during operations.

**2** A drill for making holes in bones or teeth.

**3** A saw for cutting through bones.

**4** Forceps and pincers to remove embedded objects such as thorns.

**5** A censer, an object used in herbal medicine to burn incense.

**6** Herbal cures inside cloth bags.

**7** Magical charms in the shape of the eye of the Egyptian god Horus.

**8** Scales for weighing herbal cures.

**9** Cups for extracting blood.

**10** A papyrus scroll.

**11** Shears for cutting hair.

**12** A sponge for cleaning wounds.

**13** Spoons for administering cures.

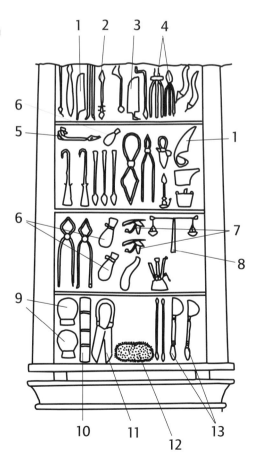

# MEDICINE MEETS SCIENCE

Pain, infection, and many deadly diseases were conquered as medicine became more scientific during the 19th century.

**At the beginning** of the 19th century medicine had not really changed since the time of the ancient Greeks. Doctors thought that bad air, the climate, or a poor diet caused diseases. They did not realize the need for cleanliness to prevent infections. Hospitals were often filthy, and patients who went in for treatment had a high risk of becoming infected and dying as a result of their stay. The most feared medical conditions were those that needed amputation—the surgical removal of a part of the body such as an arm or leg. At that time there was no effective pain relief for operations, and patients were usually tied down to the operating table

▲ *Medical researchers apply scientific principles to solve the many mysteries of medicine that still exist, such as the causes of cancer and the processes of ageing.*

## KEY COMPONENTS

### Hypodermic syringe

Before the 19th century, all medicine was administered by mouth. Then, around 1850, French surgeon Charles Gabriel Pravaz (1791–1853) and Scottish doctor Alexander Wood (1817–84) independently began injecting morphine beneath the skin using a syringe, a glass tube, and a plunger with a hollow metal needle. Pravaz and Wood found that this new method enabled them to control doses much more accurately. The drug also acted much faster and could be injected at the site where pain was worse. Before long, news of the invention traveled and use of hypodermic (literally "under the skin") syringes became widespread. Today, glass tubes have been replaced with plastic ones. They have a scale marked so drug doses can be measured accurately. Modern syringe needles are disposed of rather than sterilized and reused.

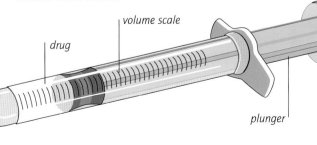

*drug*

*volume scale*

*plunger*

*needle*

after being forced to drink massive amounts of alcohol. During the century medical treatment became much safer due to the work of several scientists who developed safe anesthetics (substances that relieve pain) and realized the value of keeping hospitals and medical equipment free from microscopic germs such as bacteria and viruses.

## Pain relief

In 1848 a patient who had suffered an amputation said that someone preparing to undergo an operation was like "a condemned criminal preparing for an execution." Fortunately, this was soon to change. In 1799 British chemist Sir Humphry Davy (1778-1829) discovered the anesthetic properties of a gas called nitrous oxide, or laughing gas. When he

## PSYCHIATRY AND PSYCHOANALYSIS

The scientific method was also applied to the study of the human mind. Toward the end of the 19th century, psychiatry—the study of mental disorders—was born. One of the earliest psychiatrists was German scientist Emil Kraepelin (1856-1926), whose work seemed to show that mental illness is caused by physical problems in the brain. In 1885 another branch of psychiatry, called psychoanalysis, was developed by Austrian Sigmund Freud (1856-1939). Psychoanalysts believe that it is caused by the mind's attempt to repress unconscious thoughts. Early psychoanalysts used a variety of methods to reveal their patients' innermost emotions. For example, Freud discussed their dreams, while Swiss psychiatrist and biologist Hermann Rorschach (1884-1922) devised a test in which the patients studied inkblot patterns and talked about what they saw.

## NURSING PROFESSION

A revolution in nursing also took place during the 19th century due, in part, to the work of Florence Nightingale (1820-1910). In 1854 the British public was horrified by news reports of the terrible hospital conditions suffered by soldiers wounded in the Crimean War (1854-1856). Nightingale and her team of 38 nurses were sent to deal with the problem and saved countless lives by improving conditions and care. On her return to England Nightingale opened a training college for nurses at St. Thomas's Hospital in London. Soon nurses were receiving far better training, and nursing became a respected profession.

▲ Florence Nightingale became famous for reorganizing the hospital wards in the Scutari Barracks in Istanbul, Turkey, during the Crimean War.

## WORDS TO KNOW

- **Anesthetic:** A chemical that renders a patient unable to feel pain.
- **Bacteria** Single-celled microorganisms that are present almost everywhere on Earth.
- **Immunize** To protect from the effects of a harmful substance or disease.
- **White blood cells:** Components of the blood responsible for destroying foreign substances and organisms.

breathed it in, he found that it made him feel so good that he burst into laughter. It also stopped the pain of having his teeth pulled out. Davy suggested that the gas might have medical uses, but his idea was largely ignored.

Scientists in the United States, Germany, and France discovered chloroform in 1831, which was also found to be an anesthetic. The liquid was first used by Sir James Young Simpson (1811–1870), a professor of midwifery (the work of helping women with childbirth) in Edinburgh, Scotland. In 1847 he gave chloroform to a woman in labor—the results were so good that in the next week he gave it to another 30 patients. However, other doctors were horrified at his using pain relief in this way because they thought that the pains of childbirth were completely natural and so should not be prevented. Simpson continued to use chloroform, but it was not widely accepted until Queen Victoria (1819–1901) decided to use it when she gave birth to her eighth child, Prince Leopold.

## CHLOROFORM INHALER

The early use of anesthetics was not without hazards. Several patients died from overdoses of chloroform. Junker's chloroform inhaler was invented in 1885 and made anesthetizing patients safer and easier to control. The anesthetic was held in a bottle, and its level could be monitored through a small window. A syringe ball was squeezed to bubble air through the anesthetic, and the resulting mixture of air and chloroform vapor passed along a rubber tube to a face mask, which was placed over the patient's mouth and nose. The hook was for attaching the device to the clothing of the person using it.

◀ Early anesthetics, such as chloroform and ether, were poured onto a cloth and inhaled from a bowl-shaped mesh held over the face.

## Microorganisms and disease

Bacteriology (the study of bacteria) also had its origins in the 19th century. The idea that microorganisms such as bacteria could cause diseases—the so-called "germ theory"—came about mainly through the work of microbiologists Louis Pasteur (1822–1895) in France and Robert Koch (1843–1910) in Germany.

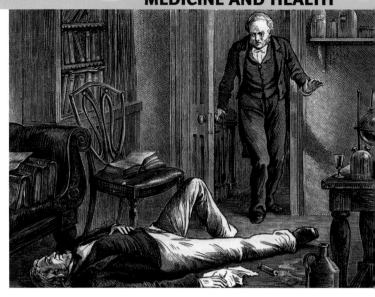

▶ *James Young Simpson is overcome during an early experiment with chloroform.*

## Early anesthesia

At first laughing gas (nitrous oxide) was used for entertainment at parties in the United States and Britain, but British scientist Humphry Davy suggested that the gas could be used in hospitals for pain relief. Davy's assistant, Michael Faraday (1791–1867), discovered the gas ether, which had a similar effect to that of laughing gas, and soon ether parties were also being organized.

Crawford Long (1815–1878), a surgeon from Atlanta, Georgia, noticed that people felt no pain when they fell over at ether parties. In 1842 he carried out the first operation using ether as pain relief: a boy called James Venable was given the gas before having cysts (lumps) cut from his neck. In 1846 U.S. dentist William Thomas Morton (1819–1868), who was studying medicine at Harvard College at the time, used ether to anesthetize a patient before a surgeon removed a tumor from his neck. The operation was a success. When Robert Liston (1794–1847), a respected British surgeon, heard of this, he

▲ *A satirical cartoon shows Humphry Davy (right, with the bellows) and doctor Thomas Garnett showing off the effects of laughing gas to scientists at London's Royal Institution in 1802.*

used ether on a butler who needed his leg amputated. He managed to remove the leg in only 26 seconds—a record time. The operation was so fast and painless that the patient was not aware that it had even started!

While working as a professor of chemistry at the University of Lille during the 1850s and '60s, Pasteur was asked by the French silk industry to find out why their silkworms were being ravaged by disease. He showed that the disease was caused by a protist (a tiny, single-celled organism) and that it could be avoided by breeding only with healthy silkworms. Earlier he had also demonstrated that some microorganisms cause foods and drinks such as wine and milk to go bad in a process called fermentation. As a result of this Pasteur went on to develop pasteurization, which involves heating and rapidly cooling fresh products to preserve them without cooking them.

▲ *Louis Pasteur used this flask in experiments into germs. The sterile broth in the flask stayed fresh because bacteria could not reach it through the swan-shaped neck, while broth exposed to air eventually went sour.*

## Cause of disease

Robert Koch went on to show that each disease was caused by one type of microorganism. He found a way of growing bacteria on a solid gel called agar and devised a set of rules that could be used to prove that a particular bacterium was causing a particular disease. In 1876 he found that a rod-shaped bacterium causes anthrax (a disease of livestock and humans). He also found the bacterium that causes tuberculosis (a lung disease) in 1882 and the bacterium that causes cholera (a tropical disease that infects the digestive system and is caught by drinking unclean water) in 1883.

◄ *The microscope was invented by Dutchman Anton Van Leeuwenhoek in the 1870s. Using this simple device he was the first person to see bacteria and other microorganisms.*

## SOCIETY AND INVENTIONS

### Smallpox—the greatest medical triumph

At the end of the 18th century smallpox had replaced plague as the biggest killer. The disease produced disfiguring pustules (sores) all over the body and nearly always killed the sufferer. However, in China doctors had learned how to give people a weak strain of the disease to protect them against the more deadly illness. By the 18th century, this idea had spread to England. In the west of England people noticed that dairy maids who caught the similar disease cowpox from milking diseased cows seemed to be immune to smallpox. In 1774 a farmer called Benjamin Jesty immunized his wife and two sons against smallpox by injecting them with a small amount of infected cowpox pus. The news of their immunity spread and eventually was heard by a British physician called Edward Jenner (1749–1823). Jenner then studied dairy workers for 20 years and in 1796 vaccinated eight-year-old James Phipps with cowpox. Six weeks later he infected James with smallpox but the boy did not catch the disease—the vaccine had made him immune to smallpox.

In 1966 the World Health Organization (WHO) announced that there would be an attempt to wipe out smallpox. More than 600 WHO workers traveled all over the world for 10 years, rushing to outbreaks of the disease. The last person to catch smallpox naturally was a three-year-old Indian girl called Rahima Banu in 1975. Treatment helped her survive. Today, the only surviving virus is kept in a few high-security laboratories.

▶ *Edward Jenner injects a child with his smallpox vaccine.*

▲ *Robert Koch works in his laboratory in the 1890s. His assistant Julius Petri invented shallow dishes for growing bacteria samples—known today as petri dishes.*

When Pasteur heard about Koch's anthrax experiments, he wondered whether it was possible to immunize (stimulate the body to protect itself) against anthrax. At this time the only disease that could be controlled by immunization was smallpox.

In 1880 Pasteur began research into rabies, a deadly disease of the nervous system. Unfortunately, he was unable to grow the organism that causes it, because it is a virus rather than a bacterium. Despite this problem, Pasteur managed to make a rabies vaccine by injecting rabbits with liquid extracted from the spinal cords of diseased animals. When the rabbits died, he dried out the spinal cords to

## FACTS AND FIGURES

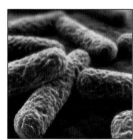

● Norwegian doctor Armauer Gerard Hansen discovered the bacterium responsible for leprosy, which damages nerves, in 1879.

● *Plasmodium,* a single-celled organism, that causes malaria was discovered by French doctor Alphonse Laveran in 1881.

● The bacterium that causes bubonic plague was first identified by Swiss-born French microbiologist Alexandre Yersin in 1894 during a plague outbreak in Hong Kong.

● The bacterium responsible for syphilis, a sexually transmitted disease, was discovered by microbiologist Fritz R. Schaudinn in 1905.

# FIGHTING INFECTION

Most 19th-century doctors did not appreciate the importance of washing their hands or equipment before treating patients. As a result open wounds often became infected, leading to amputations. Joseph Lister (1827–1912), a British surgeon who had read Pasteur's work, knew that infection could be reduced by introducing sterile (germ-free) conditions to hospitals. Lister decided to use carbolic acid as an antiseptic (a substance that kills germs), because it was already used to kill bacteria in sewage. His first antiseptic operation was performed in 1865 on an 11-year-old boy who had suffered a multiple leg fracture after being run over by a cart. Lister washed the wound with carbolic acid and wrapped it in tin foil. Except where the skin was burned by the acid, the leg healed completely. At first, other doctors dismissed Lister's ideas. However, he went on to develop a weaker carbolic acid spray, which he used in 1871 in an operation on Queen Victoria.

His methods became more and more fashionable and were widely adopted.

While antiseptics made surgery much safer, the harsh chemicals used to kill germs also irritated the skin and eyes of the patient, surgeons, and nurses. A better solution, pioneered by German surgeon Ernst Bergmann, was to stop germs from reaching the patient in the first place. In this approach, called aseptic surgery, everything in the operating theater had to be thoroughly cleaned before the patient came in. The surgeon's hands and clothes were thoroughly scrubbed, and surgical instruments were placed in a chamber and treated with very hot steam to kill any germs. The sterile gloves, masks, and gowns worn by modern surgeons were invented by U.S. surgeon William S. Halsted.

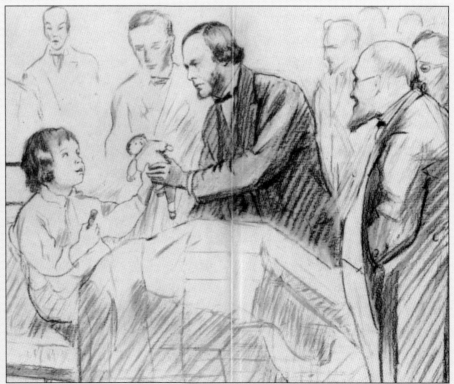

▼▶ *Joseph Lister pioneered his antiseptic techniques in the Glasgow Royal Infirmary in Scotland. He performed surgery in a shirt, vest, and bowtie.*

▲ *Italian soldiers hold people in a quarantine camp during a cholera epidemic in the 19th century after doctors had discovered how the disease was spread. The internees were given clean water and fresh fruit.*

weaken the virus. Although he tested the vaccine on dogs, he was unsure about its safety and reluctant to try it on humans. But in 1885 a nine-year-old boy called Joseph Meister, who had been badly bitten by a rabid dog, was brought to him. The boy would die without treatment, so Pasteur decided to try the vaccine. The treatment took 14 days, and the boy survived.

The work of Pasteur and Koch also led to great developments in public health. As it became obvious that epidemics of disease could be prevented by cleanliness, cities were provided with better sanitation, and slums were cleared. The problems of overcrowding caused by the Industrial Revolution were first tackled in Britain, and the other European countries soon followed.

## PASTEUR'S EXPERIMENT

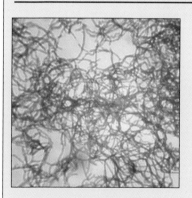

▲ *Anthrax bacteria attack livestock but can also kill people.*

In a famous experiment in 1881, Louis Pasteur injected 24 sheep, one goat, and six cows with his new vaccine, made up of anthrax bacteria that had been made weak and inactive by growing them at a raised temperature of 108°F (42°C). Two weeks later he injected his vaccinated animals and a similar number of unvaccinated animals with active anthrax bacteria. Two days after this all the vaccinated animals were still healthy, while the unvaccinated ones were dead or dying. The dramatic success of this experiment sealed Pasteur's fame and confirmed his theory that germs were the cause of disease.

# Vaccination

The body is constantly being attacked by disease-causing organisms (pathogens), such as bacteria and viruses, which it fights using a process called the immune response. In addition to fighting the pathogen, the body generates memory cells that enable it to detect and destroy that type of pathogen even quicker in the future. Vaccination exploits this feature of the immune response.

**1** A doctor or nurse injects a vaccine, which is made up of pathogens that have been made harmless in some way, into the patient's bloodstream. A small proportion of the patient's white blood cells have receptors that can bind to this pathogen.

**2** The white blood cells that have bound to the pathogen divide rapidly into antibody-producing plasma cells and memory cells. The plasma cells release large numbers of antibodies into the blood.

**3** The antibodies bind to the remaining pathogens to form clumps, which are absorbed and destroyed by macrophages, another type of white blood cell.

**4** The memory cells may remain in the body for many years. If the real pathogen is ever met, they divide more quickly and make even more antibodies than before to destroy it. This is called the secondary immune response.

## Immune response

1 

*vaccine*

*white blood cell*

Vaccine is detected by the immune system.

2

The immune system makes antibodies.

*macrophage*

3

A memory cell stores antibodies for the future.

Antibodies collect the vaccine and destroy it.

*pathogen*

4

When the real pathogen enters the body, the memory cells release the antibodies, which prevent the disease from taking hold.

▶ *A diagram represents how a vaccine primes the body's natural immunity system to prepare for attack by a disease.*

# DRUGS

Drugs are substances that have a particular effect on the way the body works, and many can be taken to treat or cure a disease.

**Some drugs are** found in foods and drinks. Caffeine is a powerful stimulant (something that increases nervous activity in the brain) and a diuretic (something that increases urine flow), and it is found in small but powerful quantities in tea, coffee, and some soft drinks. Alcohol is a drug and can cause serious illnesses if taken in large amounts. The nicotine in tobacco smoke is a drug, a highly addictive one. Although it causes many illnesses, smokers find it very hard to stop using it. Medical drugs are therapeutic: they make the body better. The antibiotic penicillin, for example, can be taken to treat infections caused by bacteria. Other kinds of

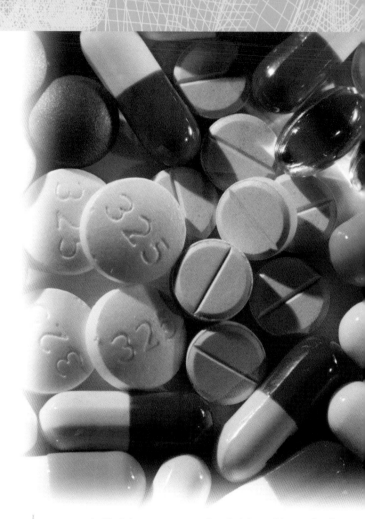

▲ Medicines are most easily administered by swallowing pills. The pills are made of harmless chalky substances that dissolve in the stomach, releasing the active ingredients.

drug, such as aspirin, are taken to relieve symptoms such as swelling and pain.

### The magic bullet

By the 1890s Paul Ehrlich (1854–1915), a German bacteriologist (a scientist who studies bacteria), had reasoned that it ought to be possible to kill germs invading the human body by using certain drugs, if only the right drug could be found. This was the so-called magic bullet theory: that a specific chemical could be used to target a particular kind of cell or microorganism.

▲ German Paul Ehrlich developed the first artificial bacteria-killing drug in the early 20th century.

# THE QUININE STORY

Legend has it that a South American, lost in the high Andes, was burning with fever. He stumbled into a stagnant forest pool and drank his fill of the bitter water to quench his raging thirst. Chemicals from the bark of nearby cinchona trees had leached into the water, giving it the bitter taste. When the man awoke from a deep sleep, his fever had gone.

Scientists have since found the that the bark of several species of cinchona trees contains a drug called quinine (named for the local name of the tree, *quina-quina*). This drug has since become a treatment for malaria, the often-fatal fever-causing disease that is passed on by blood-sucking mosquitoes. Quinine is also the flavoring in tonic water.

▶ *Malaria is spread by the female* Anopheles *mosquito, which sucks human blood.*

In the 16th century Spanish conquerors came to South America. They were in search of gold but they end up finding one of the most useful drugs in modern medicine. The invaders saw that Native Americans chewed cinchona bark to control fever. Spanish Jesuit priests brought back the tree bark to Europe in the 1630s, when it became widely used as a malaria treatment in Europe. Tonic water was drunk by British colonialists in India and Africa to ward off the disease. It was not until 1820, however, that French chemists Pierre Joseph Pelletier (1788– 1842) and Joseph Bienaimé Caventou (1795–1877) isolated quinine from the tree's bark.

During World War I (1914–1918) quinine was used to treat soldiers. At this time supplies to Germany were cut off and, so, in the 1920s German chemists developed artificial quinine. They devised one form, called quinacrine, and then a better form, called chloroquine. Several other synthetic forms of quinine have since been made. The parasite that causes malaria gradually becomes resistant to most forms of synthetic quinine, however, and new forms have to be devised. Quinine, the natural substance, does not encourage resistance in the same way and so is still used in the battle against malaria.

◀ *Medicinal chemicals are most concentrated in the bark of cinchona plants. As well as quinine, the plant produces quinidine, used to help unhealthy hearts beat regularly.*

## SOCIETY AND INVENTIONS

### The Pill

One group of drugs that has had a big impact on society in the last 50 years is contraceptive pills, often called simply the "Pill." Taken daily for three or four weeks in every month (depending on the type of pill), they can prevent pregnancy. The Pill was first devised in the late 1950s. It contains synthetic progesterone (progesterone is a chemical produced in a pregnant woman), which stops a woman releasing eggs from her ovaries. Many experts see the Pill as one of the key factors that led to major social changes in Western societies in the 1960s. Women's ability to decide whether or when to have children was to have great impact on their ability to take greater control of their lives.

Ehrlich was particularly concerned with syphilis, a disease transmitted by sexual contact. He decided to look for a synthetic (artificial) chemical that could be injected into a patient to kill the bacteria that cause syphilis. His Japanese assistant Sahachiro Hata (1873–1938) tested over 600 chemicals before finding the one that could do the job. This substance was marketed as Salvarsan in 1910 and was the first synthetic "magic bullet." Although Salvarsan did work, it required a series of painful injections before treatment was complete. Taking penicillin tablets was later to prove a much more effective form of treatment for syphilis.

### The sulfonamides and penicillin

In the 1920s and 1930s many scientists sought other magic bullets that could be used against common, life-threatening, infectious lung diseases such as pneumonia and tuberculosis (TB). Unfortunately, many chemicals that seemed to be likely candidates proved to be

## HERBALISM

Drugs have been with us for thousands of years. The ancient Chinese practiced herbalism (using plants for medical purposes) over 5,000 years ago. By about 1500 B.C. the ancient Egyptians were using tree resins and plant saps to treat many things. Undoubtedly, some of these remedies worked and are still used today, although others, such as giving patients a poisonous herb called hellebore to make them vomit, were positively harmful. A book written by ancient Greek physician Pedanius Dioscorides (c. A.D. 40–90) mentions more than 500 herbal remedies. In the so-called Dark Ages of Western civilization, between about A.D. 500 and 1100, progress in medical science passed to Eastern cultures. Islamic doctors added to the list of medicinal herbs found to be useful, and alchemists—the first chemists—found better ways of extracting, purifying, and administering drugs so that treatments were more effective. It was not until the 19th century, however, that the use of drugs began to approach being an exact science.

# THE TRANSMISSION OF MALARIA

Malaria is caused by several strains of a tiny single-celled parasite called *Plasmodium*. The disease is spread by the bites of female mosquitoes that suck human blood.

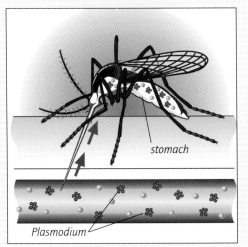

**1** *A mosquito bites an infected person, picking up some of the malaria parasites with the blood it sucks. The* Plasmodium *multiplies in the mosquito's stomach.*

stomach

Plasmodium

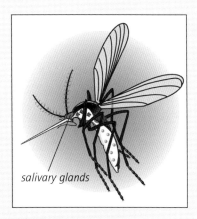

salivary glands

**2** *The* Plasmodium *migrates to the mosquito's salivary glands.*

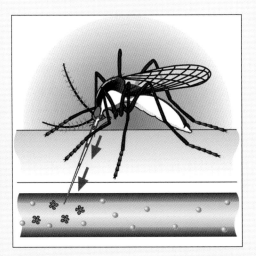

**3** *When the mosquito bites another person, the* Plasmodium *parasites enter that person's bloodstream with the mosquito's saliva.*

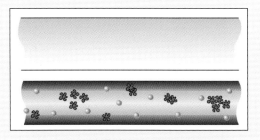

**4** *The* Plasmodium *travels to the liver, where it multiplies and forms clumps of parasites. These clumps burst and release new* Plasmodium *cells, which invade red blood cells, multiplying again. The red blood cells rupture, causing an attack of fever and releasing even more* Plasmodium *(shown left) that infect further red blood cells. The cycle of invasion, multiplication, and rupture goes on, causing periodic bouts of high fever.*

The best way to protect against malaria is to prevent mosquitoes biting. The mosquitoes are active at night, so sleeping under a net will stop the insects from getting to you. Repellent chemicals spread on the skin will also stop the insects from biting. Anti-malarial drugs kill the *Plasmodium* if a mosquito does bite.

harmful to human cells or did not work well once bacteria had started to multiply inside the body. In 1932 German bacteriologist Gerhard Domagk (1895–1964) discovered a red dye called prontosil that killed a bacterium which causes blood poisoning. In the late 1930s French, British, and U.S. researchers developed a range of related drugs (called sulfonamides, or

▲ *Alexander Fleming discovered penicillin by accident after letting his experimental equipment go moldy.*

sulfa drugs) that were effective against bacterial diseases. These drugs were at the forefront of disease treatment during the early 1940s, until antibiotics such as penicillin replaced them just after World War II (1939–1945).

British bacteriologist Sir Alexander Fleming (1881–1955) is the famous name linked with the discovery of penicillin, the first antibiotic—a natural substance produced by a fungus that kills or immobilizes bacteria. One day Fleming, casually glancing at some plates used for growing bacteria, noticed that a mold was on one of the plates. In an area around the mold there were no colonies of bacteria. It was as if the mold were producing something that was keeping bacteria at bay. In a series of experiments Fleming showed that the *Penicillium* mold produced a substance that could kill the bacteria responsible for several common and dangerous bacterial infections, including meningitis (inflammation of the linings and coverings of the brain).

Fleming went on to show that the substance, which he called penicillin, was not

## ALL IN THE MIND

Before the 1950s there were no drugs for treating mental illness. In the late 1940s French surgeon Henri Laborit was seeking a drug that could calm anxious patients just before they had surgery. He found chlorpromazine to be a highly effective drug for the purpose. French psychiatrists Jean Delay and Pierre Deniker soon found chlorpromazine to be very effective in calming patients suffering from two mental illnesses called schizophrenia and manic depression. Chlorpromazine was the first of half a dozen or so drugs that can control the extreme behavior of mentally ill patients, so allowing them to leave the hospital and live in the community. By the late 1960s hundreds of thousands of mentally ill people in the United States alone had been successfully released from the hospital under a drug-care program.

◀ *Drugs can change the way people think and how they feel by reducing anxiety or paranoia.*

harmful to laboratory animals such as mice.
He even used some mold extract to successfully
treat a colleague's eye infection.

Fleming did not investigate the drug further.
That was left to scientists at Oxford University
in England led by British biologist Sir Howard
Florey (1898–1968) and German-born
biochemist Ernst Chain (1906–1979). Between
1939 and 1940 they succeeded in purifying

▶ *Antibiotics are commonly given to infants as their*
*bodies are more at risk from attack by bacteria.*

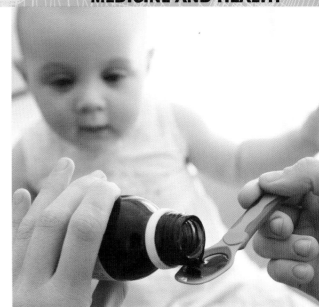

## SCIENTIFIC PRINCIPLES

### Antibiotics

There are two types of antibiotic, each
of which has a different way of
attacking disease-causing bacteria.
Bacteriostatic antibiotics prevent
bacteria from growing, which gives
the body's immune system time to kill
them and eradicate the infection.
Bactericidal antibiotics, such as
penicillins, actively kill the bacteria.

**1** Bactericidal antibiotics destroy
bacteria by attacking their protective
cell walls. This keeps the cells from
maintaining their outer barriers, which
then begin to disintegrate.

**2** This allows water to flood
into the bacteria.

**3** The water eventually causes the
bacteria to swell and explode.

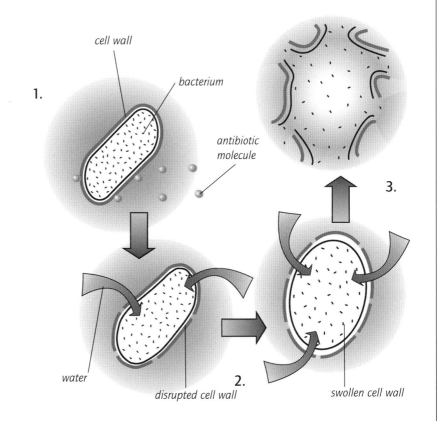

penicillin and testing its effectiveness in mice and people. They could make only tiny quantities of the drug, however, and money and resources were scarce because it was wartime. They went to the United States to get the funds needed to make penicillin in large quantities. Toward the end of the war in Europe, in 1944, there were sufficient supplies of penicillin to treat all injured Allied soldiers who were in danger of infection.

Penicillin was soon found to be effective against a wide range of bacteria, including those common forms that caused blood poisoning. Dozens of other antibiotics have been found in all kinds of microorganisms, and new

▼ *Meadowsweet produces a natural version of aspirin.*

## FACTS AND FIGURES

● Aspirin was the first truly synthetic drug, developed in the 1890s.

● It is used to fight pain and swelling, to lower fever, and to thin the blood (which helps prevent heart attacks), and it might even help prevent bowel cancer.

● In 1997, doctors found that on very rare occasions aspirin caused Reye's Syndrome, a brain disorder in children. As a result, children under 12 should not be given aspirin.

ones have also been manufactured artificially. However, there is a down side to this treatment. Antibiotics have been used in such a widespread manner—even routinely being put in animal feed to prevent farm animals getting infections—that many bacteria are now becoming resistant to some antibiotics. Scientists have to find or devise new antibiotics to keep one step ahead of the microorganisms. If they cannot, there is a danger that we will be returning to the days before antibiotics, when there was nothing to kill the most dangerous bacteria.

### Killing pain

As well as tackling disease, many drugs have been developed for treating everyday pain, such as headaches, toothache, and arthritis (inflammation of the joints). In the 1820s Swiss scientist Johann Pagenstechter found a painkilling substance—later described as salicylic acid by German chemist Karl Jacob Lowig—in the meadowsweet plant. The structure of this new drug was discovered in 1853 by Charles Frédéric Gerhardt (1816–1856), a chemistry professor at Montpellier University in France. Unfortunately, it badly irritated the stomach lining and was only used by people whose pain was severe enough to warrant the side effects.

One user was Herr Hoffman, who lived in Germany and had terrible arthritis. His son, Felix Hoffman, was a chemist at the Bayer Drug Company, and he decided to change the drug to help his father. He came up with a new drug called acetylsalicylic acid, which gave his father his first pain-free night in years. In 1899 this

▶ *Drugs such as aspirin, acetaminophen, and ibuprofen, which ease headaches and other minor pains, are available to buy without needing permission from a doctor.*

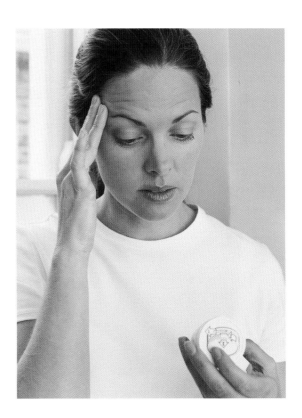

## THE THALIDOMIDE TRAGEDY

◀ *Many thalidomide-damaged children died soon after birth. The survivors generally had deformed arms and legs.*

In the 1950s Wilhelm Kunz, a chemist working at Chemie Grunenthal in Germany, invented a substance called thalidomide, which seemed to be the ideal sleeping tablet. It worked well and seemed to have few, if any, side effects. However, in the late 1950s reports of side effects began to come in, and then, in 1961, Australian physician William

McBride reported the tragic news that some pregnant women who had taken thalidomide in early pregnancy had given birth to children with deformed arms and legs. By the end of 1962 the drug had been withdrawn, but not before 7,500 thalidomide children had been born worldwide. The episode triggered a strengthening of the procedures for testing new drugs. In the United States, an important drugs bill was passed by Congress in 1962. Strangely, thalidomide may be making a comeback. In 1989 the drug was shown to exist in two forms, one that has the sedative (sleep-inducing) effect and the other that is responsible for birth defects. Thalidomide is now used, under controlled conditions, for treating leprosy (an infection that causes nerve damage), cancers, and immune disorders (malfunctions of the body's defense system).

▲ *New drugs are tested on animals before they are given to human subjects. Blood tests and other observations are taken to check if the drug is causing harm.*

drug was given the name aspirin. Aspirin was the most popular painkiller until the 1980s, when acetaminophen took over.

## Finding new drugs

Drug companies use four main methods in their search for tomorrow's wonder drugs. The first is to imitate or use a natural substance that is already believed to be useful. Today there are few opportunities for this because the majority of traditional remedies have already been studied. A second approach involves copying an existing drug but changing its design slightly in the hope of making it even better.

A third approach is to design tailor-made drugs, working from knowledge about how the body works. The fourth method is simply to screen thousands of organisms for medically useful chemicals. Today drug companies scour tropical rainforests and coral reefs in search of plants and animals containing unusual

chemicals that could be used in medicine. However, finding such substances yields both a promise and a threat. If an anticancer drug is found in a coral reef sponge, for example, and the chemical proves to be very effective, there is then the problem of how to produce the drug in large quantities without driving the sponge to extinction. Devising synthetic chemicals that are similar to natural ones is often seen as the way ahead. An alternative is to use genetic engineering techniques in which one easily grown organism produces the chemicals needed.

Increasingly effective drugs are continually being developed for diseases such as AIDS and cancer, and there is even a chance that one day gene-therapy techniques can provide cures for genetic (inherited) diseases.

▼ *Working with substances with unknown effects is risky, so researchers protect themselves from exposure while they investigate chemicals that might be therapeutic.*

## KEY COMPONENTS

### A hospital pharmacy

The table below lists some of the main drugs found in a typical hospital. They come in a variety of forms: tablets dissolve in the digestive system, and their active ingredients are absorbed by the body. For more immediate or local effect, injections are used. Sprays, inhalers, creams, and suppositories (which are inserted through the anus) can also be used.

| Type | Role | Action |
|---|---|---|
| Analgesics  | • Nonnarcotic analgesics (such as aspirin and ibuprofen) give short-term relief of moderate pain.<br>• Narcotic, or opiate, analgesics (such as codeine and morphine) give short- or long-term relief of severe pain. | • Nonnarcotic analgesics stop the pain response at the sites of inflammation.<br>• Opiates suppress the brain's ability to register pain but also cause sleepiness. |
| Anesthetics  | • General anesthetics eliminate all sensory perception, so patients can undergo major operations while unconscious, feeling no pain.<br>• Local anesthetics eliminate sensory perception in one area, allowing, for example, a dentist to painlessly extract a tooth. | • General and local anesthetics suppress the nervous system. 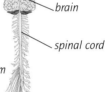<br>*brain*<br>*spinal cord*<br>*central nervous system* |
| Antibiotics and sulfa drugs  | • Fight bacteria that cause diseases. | • Antibiotics work either by killing bacteria or by preventing them from multiplying. |
| Antitumor drugs | • Treat cancers (unrestrained growth of cells), for example, after surgery to remove a tumor or during chemotherapy (the treatment of cancer using drugs).  *cancer cells* | • Antitumor drugs kill all cells that are dividing, including cancer cells but also healthy cells, for example, in bone marrow, giving these drugs considerable side effects. |
| Depressants  | • Tranquilizers reduce tension and worry.<br>• Sedatives make people sleepy. | • Depressants decrease activity of the nervous system but can be addictive. |
| Immuno-suppressant drugs  | • Prevent autoimmune ("self"-inflicted) disorders in which people's white blood cells—their immune system—attack harmless cells in the body, causing damage.<br>• Help prevent rejection of transplants. | • Immunosuppressants interfere with the production and activity of white blood cells, and so they can also increase the risk of infection and the development of cancers. |

# DIAGNOSIS AND TESTING

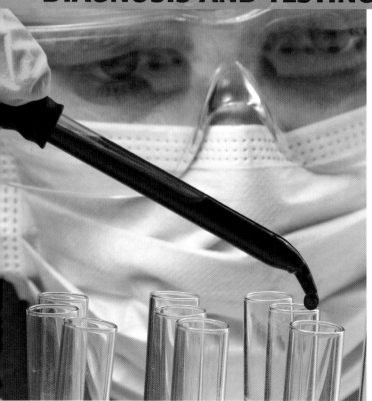

In 12th-century Europe ideas about diagnosing and treating disease had changed little from ancient Greek and Roman times. The theory of the four humors was still used as a framework for diagnosis, although it had now changed into the theory of complexion, or temperament. A person with too much black bile, for example, was melancholic (sad or depressed). As in Greek and Roman times, diagnosis could take time. European physicians would listen to their patients' stories, feel for the pulse, and sometimes make a detailed physical examination. Treatments included being given herbal remedies to make the person vomit and so get rid of black bile, or controlled bleeding to draw off excess blood and so restore the balance of the humors.

## Slow development

More sophisticated forms of diagnosis were slow in coming. It was only in the 17th century that the first microscopes were made. The early ones, such as those used by Italian biologist Marcello Malpighi (1628–1694), professor of medicine in Pisa, Italy, could show the tiny blood vessels called capillaries. It would still be nearly 200 years before the pioneering work of French chemist and microbiologist Louis Pasteur (1822–1895) and German bacteriologist Robert Koch (1843–1910) would identify specific microorganisms such as bacteria and protists (tiny, single-celled organisms) seen through a microscope, and link them to particular diseases.

**Diagnosis is the process of deciding the nature and cause of a person's ill health. In ancient times diagnosis was often a hit-and-miss affair, based as much on luck as on judgment. Today diagnoses tend to be much more accurate and reliable.**

**By 400 B.C.,** Chinese medical practitioners were trained in the art and science of diagnosis. In diagnosing an ailment, Chinese physicians felt for 12 pulses—6 in each wrist; this method is still used by many traditional Eastern doctors today. Doctors saw illness as an imbalance between two forces—the yin (dark, moist energy) and the yang (bright, dry energy). Medical conditions were often treated with acupuncture (the insertion of needles at specific points on the body) or herbalism (the use of plant chemicals).

## SOCIETY AND INVENTIONS

### Bodily balanced

Doctors in ancient India thought that the body consisted of four substances, blood (*rakta*), phlegm (*kapha*), bile (*pitta*), and wind (*vayu*). All diseases were caused by imbalances of these mysterious substances. By the third century B.C. this idea was taken, along with those of the early Egyptians, and modified by the ancient Greeks in their theory of the four humors. Greek doctors saw a person's state of health as resulting from the balance of the humors corresponding to the four basic elements of nature: blood carried air; yellow bile was filled with fire; black bile contained earth; and phlegm was full of water. Each humor and element had particular properties. Phlegm, for example, was linked with cold and damp. Too much phlegm, brought on by cold weather, was thought to give rise to colds and flu. Treatment involved keeping the patient warm.

▶ *Warm oil is trickled on the head during an Indian head massage, meant to relax and rebalance the body.*

## SOCIETY AND INVENTIONS

▼ *Just looking may tell a doctor if a sore throat needs treatment.*

### The human touch

Today's doctors have advanced medical technology, helping them make accurate diagnoses. Tissue samples can be taken and viewed through high-power microscopes. Specimens can be taken, and any microorganisms they contain grown for identification. Body fluids can be analyzed for their detailed chemistry, and the body itself can be scanned. However, a doctor often makes the first diagnosis by examining a patient and asking questions. Today computer databases and decision-making programs can help doctors make an accurate diagnosis. But, we hope, these artificial aids will never replace the doctor's human touch.

Another problem was the lack of understanding about body chemistry. The best way of diagnosing many conditions would later be found to be by analyzing substances in the body. Protein in urine, for example, may be a sign of kidney problems. At the end of the 18th century chemistry was still in its infancy, and it would not be until well into the 19th century

## HEART AND BRAIN WAVES

By the early 20th century scientists and physicians were eager to measure any physical and chemical features of the body that might prove useful in diagnosing damage or disease. In 1903 Dutch scientist Willem Einthoven (1860-1927) performed the first electrocardiograph (ECG)—a recording of the electrical activity of the heart. The apparatus he used, called a string galvanometer, was very bulky, but by 1928 portable devices were being used that weighed only 30 lb (14 kg). In the 1920s German biologist Hans Berger (1873-1941) used a string galvanometer to detect brain waves. This led, by the early 1940s, to the development of electroencephalograms (EEGs)—recordings of brain activity that are used to diagnose epilepsy and detect brain injuries.

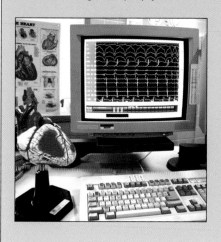

◄ The electrical activity of a heart can be displayed and analyzed on computer.

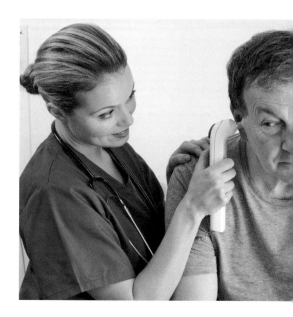

▲ A doctor measures the temperature of a patient using a digital thermometer placed in the ear. This device gives an accurate reading in a few seconds.

that scientists could begin to investigate what happens to chemicals when they enter the body.

### Signs and symptoms

Despite limitations in making diagnoses, European medicine had become much more scientific by the end of the 18th century. Doctors were carrying out experiments. They made detailed observations and kept careful records of a patient's signs (what the doctor can see or measure) and symptoms (what the patient tells the doctor about how they feel). The Industrial Revolution in the late 18th and early 19th century led to the development of new ways to work with metal and glass, and opportunities arose to develop new kinds of instruments for diagnosing medical conditions.

In spite of developments in instrument making, the clinical thermometer—the device used to measure body temperature—was surprisingly slow in coming. Various Italian scientists developed bulky thermometers in the late 16th century. Among them was Italian astronomer Galileo Galilei (1564–1642), better known for his ideas about the Solar System. In the early 18th century German physicist Daniel Gabriel Fahrenheit (1686–1736) devised his famous temperature scale. However, it was not until 1867 that British physician Sir Thomas Clifford Allbutt (1836–1925) devised the first small mercury thermometer that registered quickly and accurately. Before this standard thermometers were more than 12 inches (25 cm) long and took 20 minutes to register. Measuring body temperature soon became a standard part of medical examination. Raised body temperature was seen as a clear sign of fever—a feature of many diseases.

◄ *An old-fashioned sphygmomanometer used to measure blood pressure.*

## ENDOSCOPES

An endoscope is an optical instrument that is passed into the body through a hole to give an inside view. Remarkably, this technique dates back to 1826, when French doctor Pierre Ségalas (1792–1875) designed a hollow, metal tube, or speculum, lit by candles for seeing inside the bladder. Refinements followed during the 19th century, but endoscopy only really came of age in the 1950s, when fiber-optic technology was developed. By 1965 Professor Harold Hopkins of Reading University, England, had developed an endoscope that produced clear, magnified images of objects at its tip.

Today's most sophisticated endoscopes are long and flexible, and contain hundreds of tiny glass strands (fiber optics) that carry light to the tip. The tip may contain a camera that transmits pictures to a screen. The tips are also equipped with tiny surgical instruments, such as forceps, to take tissue samples to aid diagnosis, scissors to cut through tissue and remove growths, brushes to take samples of cells for analysis, and lasers for burning off unwanted growths. Water-and-air-supply tubes allow the doctor to wash and dry the tissues being investigated.

Once diagnosis is complete, an endoscope may be used to carry out the surgery itself. This type of operation—called keyhole, or noninvasive, surgery—minimizes damage to surrounding tissues and allows patients to recover more quickly than after normal surgery.

▲ *A surgeon feeds a drainage tube into an endoscope. The handle holds several switches for controlling the tool at its flexible tip.*

▲ *René Laënnec, the inventor of the stethoscope, listens to the internal organs of a patient in the early 19th century.*

### Seeing inside the body

Auscultation (listening to breathing and heart sounds through the chest cavity) is a diagnostic method that dates back to ancient Greek times. Today the familiar tubular rubber device with cup and earpieces is called the stethoscope. The first use of a stethoscope is believed to have been by French physician René Laënnec (1781–1826) in 1816. It happened, so the story goes, when he was listening to the heart sounds of an extremely large lady. Rather than press his ear directly against her chest, he rolled a sheaf of paper into a cylinder and listened to her heart sounds through this. It was surprisingly effective. He soon replaced the paper model

with a wooden device. In 1852 U.S. physician George P. Cammann (1804–1863) improved on the basic design by adding tubes and earpieces, one leading to each ear.

In November 1895 German-born Dutch physicist Wilhelm Röntgen (1845–1923) discovered X rays—highly penetrating electromagnetic radiation. As early as 1898 the British Army was using a mobile X-ray unit in Sudan to find bone fractures in injured soldiers.

Scientists have developed many new scanning technologies. Ultrasound scans use very high-pitched sound waves, which echo off internal body structures. The first ultrasound images of structures inside the body were produced by U.S. physician Robert Lee Wild in 1952. A few years later British physician Ian Donald (1910–1987) used ultrasound to see an unborn child in the uterus.

▼ *A doctor uses an early X-ray device to look inside a patient's chest. X rays are shining from behind the patient, through the body, and show up on the light-sensitive plate.*

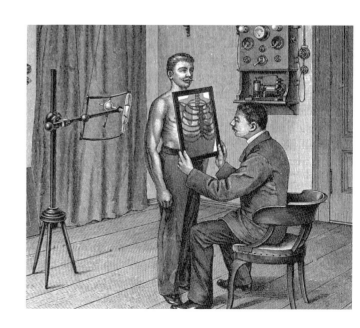

## SCIENTIFIC PRINCIPLES

### Ultrasound

Sound waves that have a higher frequency than the sounds that humans can hear are ultrasound waves. Ultrasound waves are reflected by small objects, forming echoes that can be used to create images of internal organs. In an ultrasound machine the transducer is often a hand-held device that is passed over the outside of the body (for example, the abdomen of a pregnant woman) to scan the insides; a layer of gel on the skin eases the transmission of waves. The transducer converts electrical energy into ultrasonic waves. Returning echoes are converted into electrical pulses by the transducer. A computer interprets the data and, according to the intensity of the pulses and direction of echoes, produces an image of the scanned object.

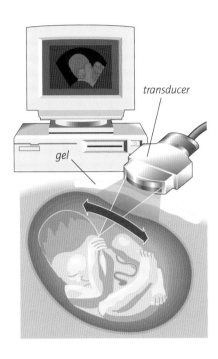

transducer

gel

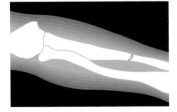

X rays

photographic plate

image on X-ray film

### X rays and computed tomography

X rays are a type of electromagnetic radiation. Because X rays darken photographic film and can penetrate places that light cannot, they can be used to produce images of bones, organs, and internal tissues. An X-ray machine produces X rays by striking a tungsten target with a beam of high-speed electrons. The beam of X rays is passed through the patient's body onto a plate of photographic film. Bones absorb a large amount of the X rays, showing up as white "shadows" on the film. Other tissues absorb fewer X rays so show up as gray areas. Computed tomography (CT) involves taking a series of X-ray pictures of cross sections, or slices, through the body. Electronic sensors detect the passage of X rays rather than photographic film, sending the data directly to a computer. The computer combines these slices of X-rayed images to produce a three-dimensional image of the organ scanned.

In 1972 U.S. physicist Allan MacLeod Cormack and Godfrey Newbold Hounsfield, a computer expert and engineer combined X-ray and computer technology. The technique they developed is called computerized tomography (CT). This method is one hundred times more sensitive than traditional X-ray technology and can detect small tumors and blood clots. CT paved the way for other scanning methods, such as positron emission tomography (PET). This technique can track brain activity from second to second and is extremely useful for researching mental illness and pinpointing brain tumors.

In 1977 U.S. physicist Raymond Damadian took the first picture inside the human body using a technique called magnetic resonance imaging (MRI). MRI does not involve X rays or radioactive substances and so is a particularly safe method. It is effective in producing an image of the damage to soft tissues such as muscles and nerves and, like PET, gives information about the biological activity of the

tissues. Unfortunately, modern scanning methods, such as PET, CT, and MRI are expensive and can only be performed in large hospitals. In poorer countries doctors continue to rely on older, less expensive methods.

## SCIENTIFIC PRINCIPLES

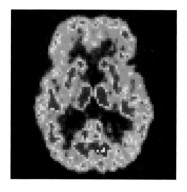

◄ PET scans show up which parts of the brain are active, so doctors can see which sections control different parts of the body.

### Positron emission tomography

Positron emission tomography (PET) involves placing the patient's head, for example, inside a ring of sensors. The patient is injected with a mildly radioactive substance that gives off positrons (positively charged electrons). The radioactive substance collects in biologically active parts of the body, such as the brain. As the positrons collide with electrons in the brain tissue, they emit gamma rays—a type of short-wave electromagnetic radiation. The sensors detect the points where these rays emerge, and a computer analyzes the data, producing images of slices of the brain that can be made into a three-dimensional image. PET scanners give information about function as well as structure—they can show, for example, which parts of the brain are active when a person is working, listening, reading, or sleeping. PET scans are often used to detect tumors and to examine brain functioning in mentally ill people.

## Magnetic resonance imaging

Magnetic resonance imaging (MRI) depends on the tendency of hydrogen atoms to resonate (wobble) and give off radio waves when they are placed in a strong magnetic field. The patient lies on a platform inside what is basically a large, hollow magnet. The angle of the platform can be adjusted to target particular areas of the body. A magnetic field is applied to the body, and this causes the protons of the body's hydrogen atoms to align themselves in the same direction like tiny magnets (normally they point in random directions). When the MRI machine emits a beam of radio waves, the protons are briefly knocked out of alignment. As they realign themselves, the protons emit faint radio signals that are picked up by the machine's radio-wave receiver. A computer analyzes this data, and according to the length and strength of the detected signals, creates a cross-sectional image of the tissues scanned. MRI can "see through" bones and organs, providing detailed images of, for example, tumors, joints, blood vessels, and the gray matter and white matter that make up the brain.

▶ A patient must not wear any metal jewelry when they enter the MRI machine. The huge magnetic forces will rip it off the body. Metallic implants inside the body would also move around causing painful internal damage.

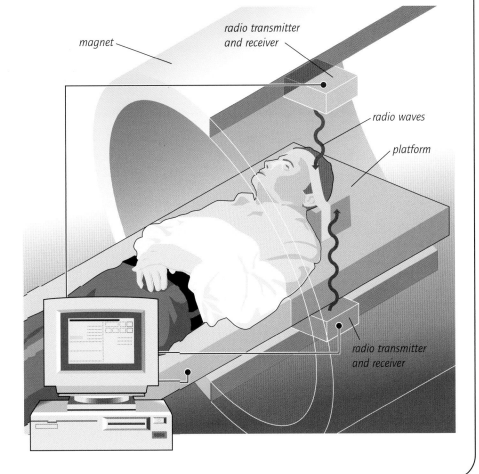

magnet

radio transmitter and receiver

radio waves

platform

radio transmitter and receiver

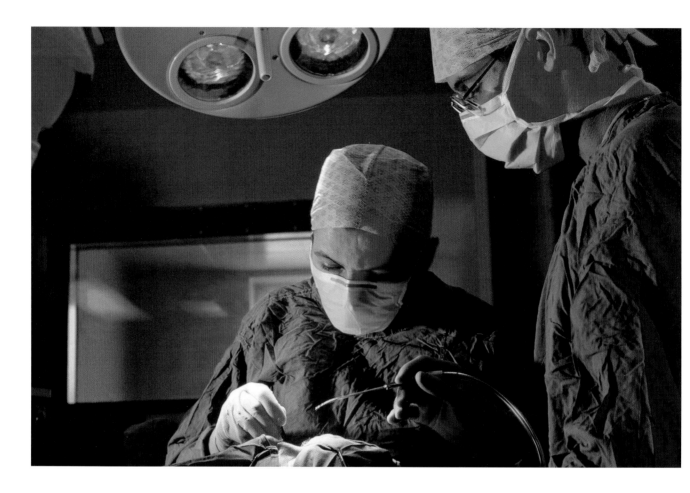

Medical practitioners have carried out surgical operations since ancient times. The first recorded surgical operation was carried out 7,000 years ago. However, even with antiseptics and anesthetics, surgery is still always risky.

**Early surgery involved** cutting off body parts and sewing up wounded soldiers. Doctors did not often cut deep into a person's body—patients would nearly always bleed to death during the operation.

One of the first successful internal operations—on the stomach—was carried out by Viennese surgeon Theodor Billroth in the

▲ Surgeons do not work alone. Nurses and other doctors help keep the patient comfortable and keep the lead surgeon supplied with the tools he or she needs.

mid-1800s, and his 1863 classic book *General Surgical Pathology and Surgery* established him as the founder of modern surgery. Today, Billroth's pioneering operation is still one of the standard treatments for stomach disorders.

During the 20th century many surgical discoveries allowed doctors to develop ways of transplanting organs and giving blood transfusions. Artificial organs and life-support systems have also revolutionized medicine and saved countless lives.

▶ *Sushruta, an Indian doctor from around 2,800 years ago, developed many surgical tools. He used eye surgery to cure blindness and even performed plastic surgery on noses.*

## The age of machines

Even before immunosuppressant drugs were developed to prevent rejection of transplanted items, doctors were desperately trying to find a way to transplant organs successfully. They were helped by the development of machines that could take over the job of the damaged organ

---

## TISSUE REJECTION

▲ *A 17th-century doctor transfuses a patient with his own blood through a tube connecting the blood vessels in their arms.*

In 1628, English scientist William Harvey (1578-1657) discovered that the body contained a fixed volume of blood. If a patient lost blood, he or she would die, so doctors used a transfusion—replacing it with the blood from another person. However, patients often suffered terrible reactions to the new blood. In 1900 U.S. scientist Karl Landsteiner (1868-1943) discovered this happened because of blood types. A patient could only receive blood of the same type as their own—any another type would cause the blood to form dangerous clots.

The immune system also attacks—or rejects—a transplanted organ. The organ is covered in protein markers called antigens, which show that it comes from outside the body. The first drug to prevent the body rejecting transplanted tissues was cortisone. This was used in 1951 to prolong the life of a skin transplant. In 1958 irradiation was used in the first successful kidney transplant between nonidentical twins. Irradiation kills the body's white blood cells, which make up the body's immune system and attack transplanted organs. The main anti-rejection drug today is cyclosporin. In 1972 Swiss scientist J.F. Borel discovered the amazing properties of this drug, which is found in a mushroom that grows in Norway.

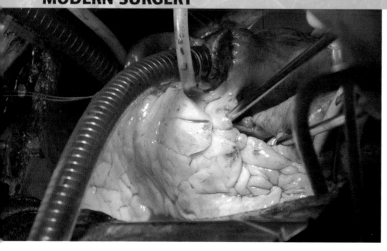

◄ *A heart is bypassed during surgery. A pumping machine is connected to the blood supply by thick tubes, so the heart can be stopped, making it easier for surgeons to fix it.*

until a donor could be found. In 1914 a team at Johns Hopkins in Baltimore invented the first artificial kidney, or dialysis machine, which they tested on dogs with kidney disease. However, these experiments were forgotten by everyone

## ABO BLOOD GROUPS AND TRANSFUSIONS

There are four blood groups: A, B, AB, and O. If a person with blood group A received blood of type B during a transfusion, the result would be fatal. People with blood group A produce anti-B antibodies, which "attack" antigen B (found on type B blood cells), making the blood clot. People with blood group AB produce neither anti-A nor anti-B antibodies, so they can receive blood of type A, B, AB, or O. People with blood group O, however, produce both anti-A and anti-B antibodies, so they can only receive type O blood. In practice matching blood types are given whenever possible, and there are other blood grouping systems—the Rhesus system, for example—that have to be considered as well as the ABO system.

| | Donor type A (anti-B antibodies) | Donor type B (anti-A antibodies) | Donor type AB (neither anti-A nor anti-B antibodies) | Donor type O (both anti-A and anti-B antibodies) |
|---|---|---|---|---|
| Recipient type A (anti-B antibodies) | Normal blood | Clotted blood | Clotted blood | Normal blood |
| Recipient type B (anti-A antibodies) | Clotted blood | Normal blood | Clotted blood | Normal blood |
| Recipient type AB (neither anti-B nor anti-B antibodies) | Normal blood | Normal blood | Normal blood | Normal blood |
| Recipient type O (both anti-A and anti-B antibodies) | Clotted blood | Clotted blood | Clotted blood | Normal blood |

Normal blood

Clotted blood

except a physician in the Netherlands called Willem Kolff. In 1943 Kolff invented a kidney dialysis machine for humans, using sausage casing for the tubes. The first kidney transplant in which the patient survived was carried out in 1950 by U.S. doctor Richard H. Lawler (1895-1982) and his coworkers.

Transplanting a heart was much more difficult. A heart must be removed and transplanted within a few hours. There is also the problem of keeping the blood moving around the body while the surgery is being performed. In 1930 U.S. surgeon John H. Gibbon (1903-1973) developed a heart-lung

## SCIENTIFIC PRINCIPLES

### Dialysis machine

Dialysis machines have to perform the jobs that kidneys normally do—they must filter the blood of waste products and remove excess fluid from the body, which is then sent to the bladder and eventually excreted as liquid urine.

**1** Blood is taken from the patient and pumped to the dialysis machine.

**2** The dialysis machine contains a fluid called dialysate, which is made up of water, salts, and other solutions.

**3** Inside the dialysis machine a membrane with tiny holes in it separates the blood from the dialysate. Wastes and excess fluid pass from the blood into the dialysate, which carries them away.

**4** The cleansed blood is then returned to the patient.

Dialysis can be performed at out-patient clinics, but it can also be done at home by the patients themselves. In another type of dialysis, pioneered in the 1970s, patients are simply attached to a bag of dialysate, and a membrane inside the body is used to filter the blood, which does not need to be pumped out of the body.

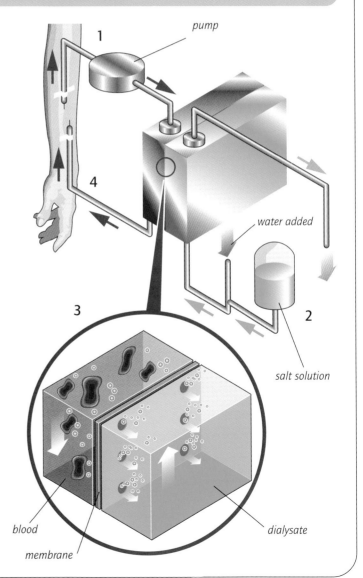

pump

1

4

water added

3

2

salt solution

blood

dialysate

membrane

### Heart-lung machine

Heart-lung machines temporarily take over the functions of the heart and lungs, allowing surgeons to carry out otherwise impossible operations in the chest. An oxygenator performs the task of the lungs—adding the vital gas oxygen to blood, which is then pumped around the body by a pump functioning as the heart. Oxygen is needed for body cells to work. The use of a heart-lung machine is limited to a few hours, since it reduces the blood supply to vital organs.

**1** Blood is taken from the main veins that bring blood to the heart from the body.

**2** This blood is oxygen-poor, and it is delivered to the artificial lung (oxygenator), where it picks up more oxygen.

**3** This oxygen-rich blood is pumped through a temperature controller and a filter (to prevent clots forming) before it is passed back to a main artery, from where it circulates around the body.

**4** Blood leaving the heart is channeled through a defoamer (to remove bubbles) and sent to the oxygenator.

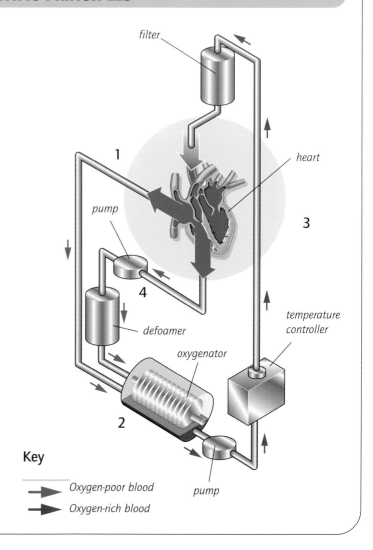

Key

Oxygen-poor blood

Oxygen-rich blood

machine that would pump oxygen into the patient's blood during heart surgery. In 1954 Gibbon used this machine to operate on a 19-year-old girl. For 27 minutes the machine kept her alive while surgeons operated on her heart.

In 1961, U.S. surgeon Norman Shumway invented a way of nourishing a new heart after it is put into the body. He used a machine to keep the patient's blood flowing after surgery

until the new heart was ready to take over. This allowed the first human-to-human heart operation to be carried out by South African surgeon Christiaan Barnard in 1967.

In addition to heart surgery the 20th century has seen the development of new ways to keep a damaged heart working. For example, pacemakers were invented in the 1950s, and in 1951 the first workable synthetic heart valve was designed and inserted into a patient by Charles Antony Hufnagel (1916–1989). In 1968 René Favaloro carried out the first coronary bypass operation. The coronary artery carries the main blood supply of the heart and can be blocked by fatty deposits—the bypass involved taking the damaged piece of artery away and replacing it with a vein cut from the patient's leg.

### Artificial body parts

Sometimes, however, even surgery cannot solve a serious heart problem. Willem Kolff began

## KEY COMPONENTS

### Pacemakers

The heart has its own electrical system, called a pacemaker, which acts to keep it beating regularly. Artificial pacemakers are implanted in the chest to send electrical impulses to the heart when its own pacemaker is not working. The first of these devices was made by Rune Elmqvist in 1958 and implanted by Swedish doctor Ake Sening in 1960. Early models had a power source under the skin and used mercury-zinc batteries, which ran out after two or three years. In 1973 a lithium-iodide power cell was developed that lasts more than six years. Modern devices use this kind of battery.

Internal pacemakers are implanted in the chest. An insulated electrical wire is inserted into the heart via a vein. A fixing mechanism such as a staple holds the electrode in place, next to the part of the heart needing stimulation. The other end of the wire plugs into the pacemaker. Electrical impulses stimulate the heart to beat. Some pacemakers discharge electrical impulses at a fixed rate; others only discharge impulses when the heart slows or a beat is missed.

connector socket

pacemaker

connector pin

pacemaker

heart

battery

electronic controls

electrical wire

heart

vein

fixing mechanism

electrode

research into developing a total replacement heart in the 1950s, and in 1957 he implanted his first model into a dog. The dog survived for 90 minutes. In 1970 Robert Jarvik devised an artificial heart made of polyurethane (a plastic) and fiber glass. This was first used in a human in 1982. The patient, Barney Clarke, survived for 112 days. The longest time a patient survived with this artificial heart was 20 months.

The most commonly used artificial body replacement is the hip. Hip replacements became possible with the development of plastics and acrylics before WWII (1939–1945), but there were problems with artificial hips until

1960. British surgeon Sir John Charnley developed a hip joint that used two different materials: the head of the femur (the long leg bone) was replaced with a stainless steel ball, and the ball of the hip joint was lined with a slippery plastic called Teflon. This allowed the new joint to move around freely in the socket.

## Revolutionizing surgery

When surgeons do not have to make large cuts to perform surgery, the patient recovers much faster. So-called minimally invasive surgery developed during the 1980s, using endoscopes equipped with lasers instead of scalpels.

## SITES OF POSSIBLE IMPLANTS

Implants are natural and artificial materials inserted into the body for medical purposes. Many implants repair or replace a part of the body that no longer works properly. The lens in an eye, for example, or even the whole eyeball, can be replaced. Pacemakers keep the heart beating regularly, and diseased heart valves can be replaced with flexible plastic ones. Hip, knee, elbow, shoulder, and finger joints can be replaced with artificial substitutes, made from metal, plastic, or ceramic. Artificial blood vessels made of synthetic materials can replace diseased sections of arteries. Implants containing radioactive materials can be inserted into tissue to treat cancers, and others containing drugs (such as contraceptives or pain killers) are inserted to release the drug slowly over a long period of time. Some implants, such as silicone breast implants, are used to improve appearance.

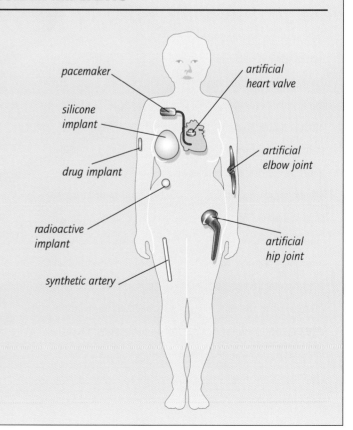

pacemaker

artificial heart valve

silicone implant

drug implant

artificial elbow joint

radioactive implant

artificial hip joint

synthetic artery

## SCIENTIFIC PRINCIPLES

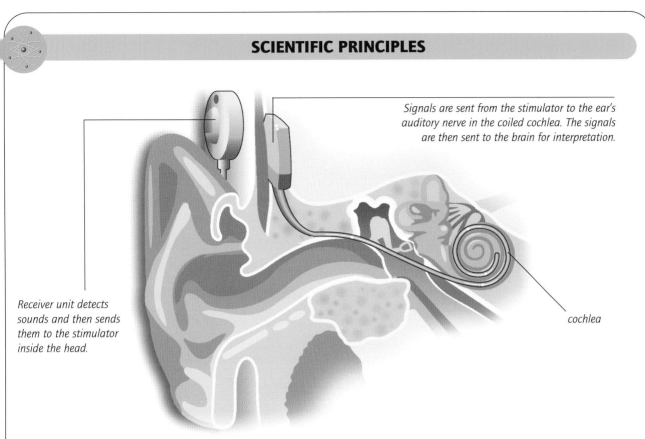

*Signals are sent from the stimulator to the ear's auditory nerve in the coiled cochlea. The signals are then sent to the brain for interpretation.*

*Receiver unit detects sounds and then sends them to the stimulator inside the head.*

*cochlea*

# Hearing aids

Most people with normal hearing imagine that people who are deaf cannot hear anything at all. In fact, this is generally not the case. A complete inability to hear, or profound deafness, affects only a small minority of deaf people. The majority have either conductive or sensori-neural hearing loss. Both of these disorders allow at least some types of sound—especially deep, booming vibrations—to be heard.

Conductive hearing loss is caused by sound being unable to pass normally from the outer to the inner ear. This may be either the result of blockage or damage to the middle ear. Conductive hearing loss causes all sounds to be heard much more quietly. Loud voices sound like whispers, while soft voices may not be heard at all.

Sensori-neural hearing loss is the result of damage to the inner ear and causes sounds to become distorted. Although less common than conductive hearing loss, it is more likely to be permanent. In most cases of sensori-neural hearing loss, high-frequency sounds are cut out. The result is that the long, rounded vowels in speech are audible but most clicking consonant sounds are not.

Hearing aids benefit people with conductive hearing loss. These tiny devices that fit in the ear work like miniature amplifiers, making quiet sounds louder to cancel out the effect of middle ear damage. People with sensori-neural hearing loss and the profoundly deaf cannot use hearing aids like this. However, they may have a cochlear implant (pictured above) fitted. This small device is surgically implanted into the inner ear. A microphone unit fitted behind the outer ear converts sounds into a simplified sound signal, which is transmitted into the head, bypassing the middle ear.

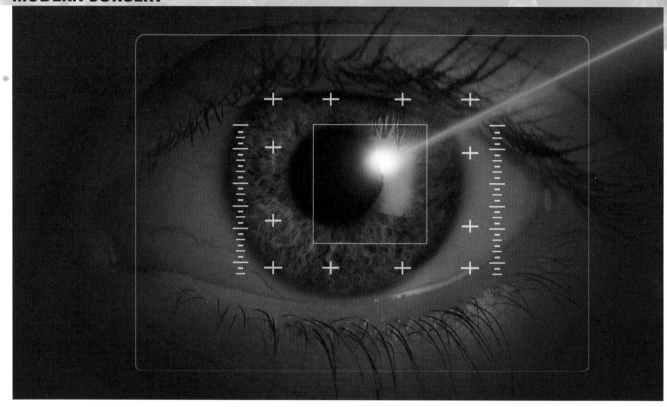

Endoscopes are sometimes put into the body through natural openings such as the mouth, but they can also be inserted through small incisions, in a procedure called keyhole surgery. Extra channels in the endoscope suck out any blood or pump in replacement fluids to flush an organ clean. Keyhole surgeons even inflate small

## FACTS AND FIGURES

- Every year in the United States around 300,000 patients are fitted with a tiny pump in the aorta (main artery of the body), which helps the heart push blood around the body. Willem Kolff invented this device in 1967.
- More than 80,000 internal pacemakers are fitted in the United States each year.

▲ *Myopia, or short-sightedness, can be cured by cutting the cornea (eye covering) with a laser. The cuts are placed precisely so they help to focus light into the eye correctly.*

balloons inside blocked arteries to push out clogs of fatty deposits.

Lasers and shock waves allow some medical conditions to be treated without the need for surgery at all. In 1982 surgeons developed a machine that can destroy kidney stones using powerful shock waves. The stones, which before this invention had to be removed by surgery, are broken down into tiny grains, which pass out through the patient's urine. In 1986 German scientist Ludwig Demling used a laser attached to an endoscope to treat gallstones. He inserted the endoscope into the gallbladder and fired laser shots at the stones to destroy them without damaging the surrounding tissue.

▶ *A surgeon operates using a robot. The doctor views the patient in virtual reality, while the robot makes precise cuts.*

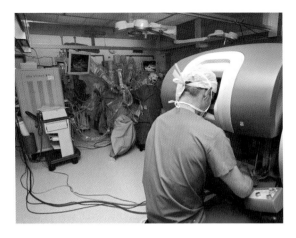

Cryosurgery (using extremely low temperatures to destroy dead, damaged, or cancerous tissue) has also revolutionized surgery. Irving Cooper, who developed a way of using liquid nitrogen, first used cryosurgery in 1960. This type of surgery is painless, and there is no risk of bleeding.

Noninvasive surgical techniques, such as the use of lasers and endoscopes, have cut drastically the amount of time needed for the surgery itself and for the patients' recovery afterward. This has led to the development of surgery on an outpatient basis, with hospital admittance, surgical operation, and discharge all sometimes occurring in just one day. As a result, most routine procedures, such as removal of the appendix or tonsils, can be performed safely with a minimum of distress to the patient.

## SOCIETY AND INVENTIONS

### Cosmetic plastic surgery

Plastic surgery is any operation that reshapes or reconstructs the body. Reconstructive surgery has a long history, treating, for example, disfiguring burns and congenital (in-born) disorders such as severe cleft palate, in which the top lip is connected to the nostrils.

Many of the techniques of modern plastic surgery originate with surgeons who were repairing the wounds and disfigurements of soldiers. Today doctors can change the shape of a person's jaw, nose, ears, breasts, and many other body parts, and they can remove excess fat, smooth out wrinkles (right), and transplant hair. But people's expectations of cosmetic surgery are often too great. It cannot produce a dramatic change in personality or cure depression that a person blames on his or her appearance.

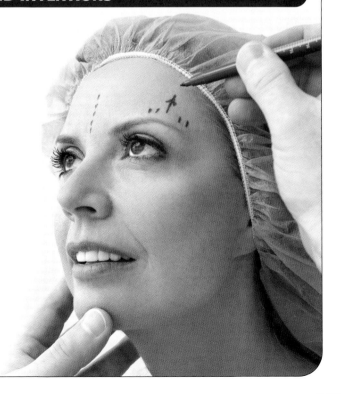

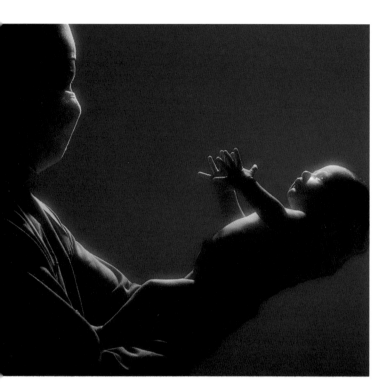

◄ In wealthy countries, most babies are born in hospital, where doctors are on hand to help if problems occur.

For much of human history, men have dominated medical practice. However, women medical practitioners have often played an important role in obstetrics, the medicine of pregnancy and birth.

**In ancient Greece** and Rome most doctors were men, but the few women who practiced medicine tended to specialize in female ailments, cared for pregnant women, and attended births. However, the best-known ancient text on gynecology was written by a man, Soranus of Ephesus, a Greek physician who lived around A.D. 100.

In the United States and Europe during the 18th and 19th centuries midwives were mostly women. However, as medicine became more scientific and technological, and more

equipment was used, male doctors began to take a much greater interest in taking control of the childbirth process. In many cultures this trend has continued right up until the present day. Many women now give birth in the hospital under the supervision of a doctor, although there have recently been moves to encourage more natural childbirth.

In the 1920s childbirth was still a very hazardous event. In the United States at least 17 percent of mothers died during childbirth. Authorities identified several factors as responsible for the high death rate, ranging from poor hygiene and housing to lack of

▼ An infant boy is circumcised a few days after birth in a Jewish ceremony in the 17th century. Judaism and Islam both require boys to be circumcised, and the procedure is also sometimes used for medical reasons.

professional care before, during, and after birth. Prenatal (before-birth) care of mother and unborn child was introduced on a wide scale.

New techniques to monitor the health of the unborn baby (fetus) were, however, slow to emerge. In the 19th century French obstetrician Adolphe Pinard designed a stethoscope to detect fetal heartbeats. He also introduced a massage technique for turning the baby into the correct head-down position for birth. In 1916 Norwegian obstetrician Christian Kielland introduced a new design of forceps for gripping the baby's head accurately to assist during

difficult births. Despite their effectiveness many doctors used them without adequate training, and in some cases they made injury to mother or baby more likely. In the 1930s the increasing use of blood transfusions helped save lives, as did the introduction of antibacterial drugs called sulfonamides. For mothers giving birth in the hospital drugs such as morphine and scopolamine were injected to ease birth pains.

The trend toward increasing technological control of childbirth continued between the 1930s and 1980s. Better forms of painkiller were developed, and epidural anesthesia

## HYGIENE SAVES LIVES

Hungarian physician Ignaz Semmelweiss (1818–1865), while working in maternity wards, noticed that mothers under the supervision of female midwives had a much better chance of surviving childbirth than those looked after by male doctors. The doctors often carried out autopsies (dissections of dead bodies to decide the cause of death), and then helped deliver babies—without washing their hands or changing their clothes! When Semmelweiss made his medical students wash their hands in disinfectant before dealing with patients, the death rate fell among childbearing women. This is an example of the use of antisepsis—methods of hygiene that kill germs, or microorganisms such as bacteria and viruses. At the time no one knew these tiny organisms were the cause of diseases, but Semmelweiss's approach worked nonetheless. It was not until about 20 years later that the famous French chemist Louis Pasteur (1822–1895) showed a link between microorganisms and disease.

▶ *Midwives have been aiding childbirth for centuries. A non-medical helper, or doula, was also sometimes present to provide companionship.*

(in which anesthetic is injected into the lower back, numbing sensation below that point) meant that mothers could stay awake during caesarean sections. A caesarean section is when the baby is delivered by surgery through the mother's abdomen.

**Controlling fertility**

Contraception has been practiced for many centuries. In ancient Egypt over 4,000 years ago women used pessaries (substances placed in the vagina) made of strange concoctions such as honey and crocodile dung. This method worked to some extent, because the concoctions made the vagina unwelcoming for active sperm. However, the method was far from foolproof, and some of the pessaries were actually dangerous. By the late Middle Ages contraception had taken an even more

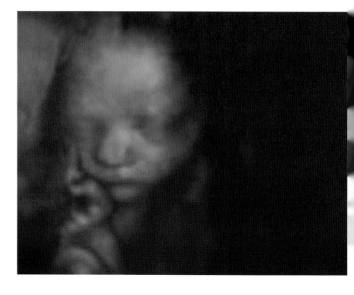

▲ *Modern ultrasound scanners can produce three-dimensional views of a developing fetus.*

▼ *A baby is delivered by caesarian section, in which surgeons cut into the womb to extract the baby once the birth canal has become blocked.*

dangerous turn, with women taking herbal mixtures to reduce fertility—the ability to conceive a child.

Italian biologist Gabriello Fallopius (1523–1562) is credited with inventing the linen condom around 1550. This was designed to

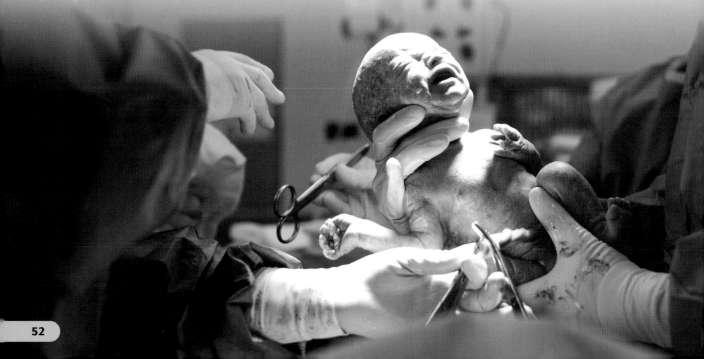

## KEY COMPONENTS

### Chromosomes, DNA, and genes

Inside the nucleus (control center) of every human body cell there are 46 chromosomes. In the male and female sex cells (sperm and eggs) there are only 23 chromosomes—so when a sperm fertilizes an egg, the resulting cell, which develops into an embryo, has the full quota of 46 chromosomes. In this way a baby inherits its chromosomes from its parents—half coming from the mother and half from the father.

Each chromosome is made up of a strand of coiled up deoxyribonucleic acid (DNA). DNA is like a twisted ladder (the double helix), the rungs of which are made up of four chemicals called bases. A gene is made up of several hundred or several thousand bases on a separated strand of the double helix. The order that the bases appear on the strand dictates which proteins are produced. Proteins are the building blocks of cells and determine every feature of a person. One faulty gene can mean a certain protein is not produced, causing a genetic disorder.

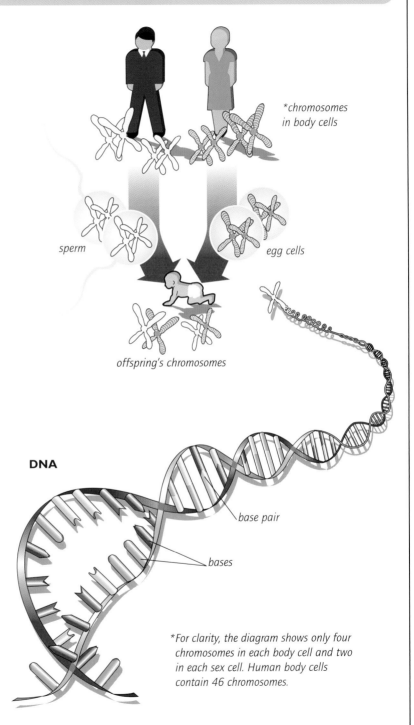

*chromosomes in body cells

sperm

egg cells

offspring's chromosomes

**DNA**

base pair

bases

*For clarity, the diagram shows only four chromosomes in each body cell and two in each sex cell. Human body cells contain 46 chromosomes.

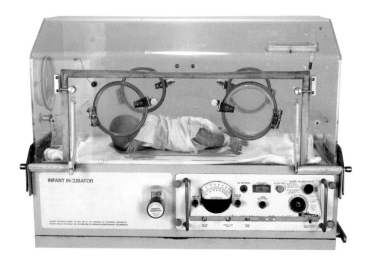

▲ *Babies that are born earlier than normal are kept in an incubator for a little while. The machine keeps them warm while they complete their development.*

prevent the transmission of sexually transmitted diseases (STDs) rather than to prevent pregnancy, although it may have worked reasonably well at combating both. Since the 1980s and the advent of HIV (human immunodeficiency virus), the disease-prevention role of the condom has returned to the fore.

German physician Frederick Adolphe Wilde made the first versions of the diaphragm in the 1820s, but in 1882 German doctor W.P.J. Mesinga devised a larger version made of latex rubber, similar to those used today. The first IUD (intrauterine device), or coil, was a silver spiral designed by German doctor Ernst Grafenberg in

1928. Today IUDs come in many shapes and sizes, and usually contain plastic and metal, and some are impregnated with the hormone progesterone to prevent the release of eggs.

Perhaps the greatest revolution in contraception came with the advent of the contraceptive pill, or the Pill. In the 1950s several chemists were involved in its early development. Progesterone—which is produced by women's bodies during pregnancy—is the Pill's main ingredient. It prevents a woman ovulating (releasing eggs). Progesterone is present in only tiny quantities in humans and other animals, but during the late 1940s U.S. chemist Russell E. Marker (1902–1984) found a way of converting substances in the wild yam plant into usable progesterone.

During the 1950s researchers developed synthetic (artificial) progesterones that were more powerful than the natural form and that could be swallowed and absorbed into the body. Between 1954 and 1959 U.S. biologists Gregory Pincus (1903–1967) and John Rock (1890–1984) tested the first contraceptive pill. By the mid-1970s more than 50 million women were using the Pill.

### Fertility treatment

There are many reasons why couples fail to have children. The woman's fallopian tubes may be blocked, or sometimes

◄ *Condoms are made from rubber. They fit over a man's penis to prevent sperm—and any disease-causing agents—from reaching the woman's uterus.*

# Contraception

For a child to be conceived, a female egg has to be fertilized by (fused with) a male sperm. Women store eggs in their ovaries, which release the eggs to travel down the fallopian tubes and into the uterus, where a baby will grow from an egg if it is fertilized. Male produce sperm in their testes, which release the sperm to travel down each vas deferens and out of the penis. During sexual intercourse the male's penis delivers sperm to the woman's vagina, and the sperm can travel past the cervix into the uterus, where an egg can be fertilized.

Contraceptive devices interfere with this process somehow, preventing conception. To prevent sperm entering the uterus, condoms can cover the penis or vagina, and diaphragms and caps are worn by women over the cervix. IUDs (or coils) make the uterus inhospitable for fertilized eggs. Women can take pills that either interfere with the release of eggs (ovulation), make the cervical mucus (thick, slimy fluid) impenetrable by sperm, or affect the lining of the uterus so that eggs cannot implant. A male Pill has been researched with the aim of preventing sperm being produced, but it has never been marketed in part due to doubts about whether it would be used. Sterilization (the cutting of each vas deferens in men and the fallopian tubes in women) is a foolproof but usually irreversible contraceptive method.

### Sites of action of contraceptive devices

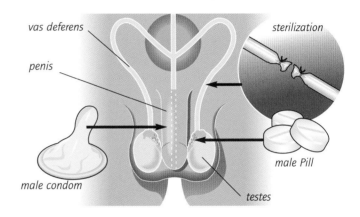

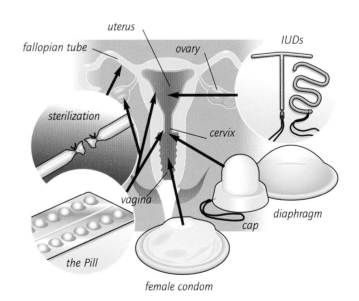

◀ Eggs, sperm and even embyros can be stored in deep freeze for several years. The freezeer uses liquid nitrogen to keep things very cold.

mucus (thick, slimy fluid) in the cervix kills the man's sperm. Or, the man may produce relatively few sperm, or those that he does produce are defective in some way. In the last 50 years many techniques have been developed to help overcome such problems

The most publicized procedure to aid fertility is the so-called test-tube baby technique, developed by British gynecologists Patrick Steptoe (1913–1988) and Robert Edwards (born 1925). This method resulted in the first test-tube baby—Louise Brown—being born in July 1978. Despite the name, test tubes are never involved, and the technique is properly called in vitro (Latin for "in glass") fertilization, or IVF. Other

## SOCIETY AND INVENTIONS

### IVF: Moral and ethical issues

The IVF technique raises many moral and ethical questions. Are the embryos (clumps of cells that will eventually develop into fetuses) growing in the dish actually human beings, or rather, are they human beings-to-be? If any of them are not replaced in the mother, should they be kept for other purposes? Unused embryos are frozen so the mother and father can use them should they wish to try again for a baby. With permission, some embryos are also experimented on, provided they are not allowed to grow beyond 14 days. However, controls on embryo experimentation vary greatly from country to country and from state to state.

▲ Fertility doctors have had a hand in the creation of millions of new lives. Without their services, many couples would not be able to have children on their own.

procedures can be used as part of IVF to help encourage fertilization if the man's sperm are of relatively poor quality. Worldwide between 1978 and 2011 over 4 million babies were conceived by IVF, but it is a difficult and costly method.

**Genetic screening**

Every cell in every living thing contains genetic (inherited) material called DNA, which carries the instructions for the development of all the characteristics of the organism. For example,

## SCIENTIFIC PRINCIPLES

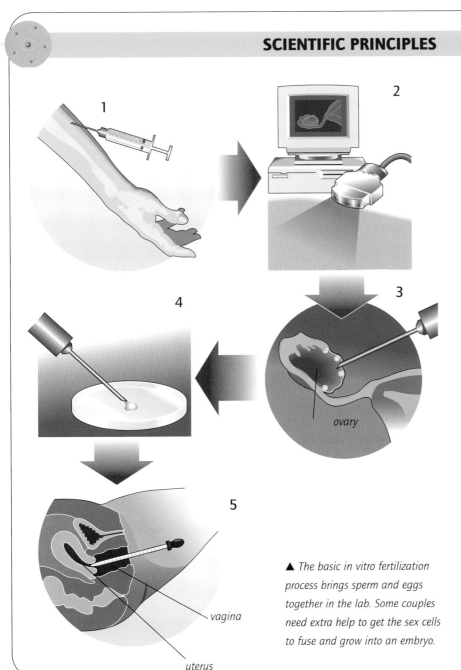

### Scientific Principles: IVF

**1** Early in a woman's menstrual cycle she is injected with fertility drugs so that she produces three or more eggs at one time.

**2** The ripening of eggs in the ovaries is monitored by a series of ultrasound scans.

**3** Immediately before ovulation (the release of eggs from the ovaries) the most ripe egg cells are removed from one of the ovaries using a fine, hollow needle.

**4** The eggs are placed in a glass dish and fertilized with her partner's sperm.

**5** Several fertilized eggs that have begun to grow into embryos (clumps of cells that grow into fetuses) are placed in the mother's uterus a few days later. If IVF is successful (success rates are less than 50 percent) it is likely that the mother will be carrying more than one child.

▲ *The basic in vitro fertilization process brings sperm and eggs together in the lab. Some couples need extra help to get the sex cells to fuse and grow into an embryo.*

whether you are short or tall, have blond or brown hair, and have blue or green eyes is determined by your DNA. Genetic screening involves examining a person's DNA to check for potential problems.

In 1952 British physician D.C.A. Bevis described amniocentesis, a technique for sampling the fluid surrounding an unborn baby and so collecting some of the baby's cells to check for genetic abnormalities. The technique is used to test for Down's syndrome, spina bifida, and other genetic conditions. Such screening methods are still very important today.

▼ *Identical twins have identical sets of genes, which makes them useful subjects in studies into the genetic causes of illnesses. If both twins develop a disease then it is likely to have been influenced by their genes.*

## FACTS AND FIGURES

● A person's DNA contains about 20,500 genes. Less than two percent of the DNA carries a code for proteins. The rest is junk or marker units between genes.

● The Human Genome Project was begun in 1990 to sequence the entire set of human DNA. The great majority of genes had been mapped by 2003, and now scientists are figuring out what each one does.

The Human Genome Project was launched in the 1990s to decipher the base sequence of every human gene and map the human genome (entire genetic material) by finding the position of each gene on particular chromosomes. The project involved hundreds of researchers working to produce a library of all human genes. The project was completed in 2003.

Studying the position and chemical nature of a human gene—and any differences between normal and faulty versions—introduces the possibility of finding out whether an individual will later be vulnerable to particular diseases, such as heart disease, cancer, or any one of hundreds of other possibilities. Some people are concerned about the use such information could be put to, however. If employers or insurance companies demanded genetic screenings, some people might find it harder to get a job or insurance if the results were not good. Also, should such people inform their family, members of which might also carry the same disease?

# GENE THERAPY

Since the mid-1980s scientists have been exploring the possibility that faulty genes can be repaired or replaced. In 1990 Ashanti DeSilva, a four-year-old girl, had white blood cells taken from her body by a U.S. medical team. Copies of a normal gene were placed in these cells to compensate for the incorrect functioning of a faulty gene, and then the cells were returned to her body. Ashanti was suffering from severe combined immunodeficiency (SCID)—a genetic disorder that meant her immune system did not work properly. The gene therapy dramatically improved Ashanti's condition.

Gene therapy has great potential, but it is still in its early stages. The biggest problems lie in getting the correct active gene to the right place in the body.

▲ A genetic "fingerprint" is a quick way of showing up a person's genetic makeup. It can be used to confirm relationships between people and to highlight if a person carries a damaging gene.

# CLONING

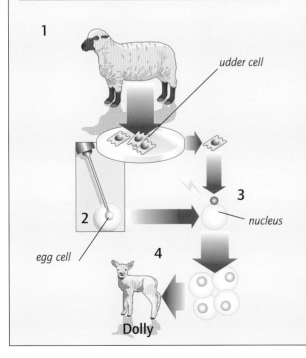

1

udder cell

2

egg cell

3

nucleus

4

Dolly

In 1996 a sheep called Dolly was born in Edinburgh, Scotland. She was the first clone—identical genetic copy—of an adult mammal.

**1** Cells were taken from the udder of an adult ewe. All the body cells of an animal have the same set of genes. As the animal develops, however, some unused genes are switched off.

**2** A sheep egg cell was prepared by having its nucleus removed.

**3** An electric current fused a nucleus from one of the udder cells with the egg cell, switching all the genes on.

**4** The cell became into an embryo, which was placed back into a ewe and grew into Dolly—a clone of the ewe from which the udder cells were taken.

It took 277 attempts to make Dolly. She died in 2003 at a much younger age than most sheep. It is unclear whether this was because she was a clone.

**430 B.C.** Greek physician Hippocrates develops a new medical technique called clinical observation.

**300s B.C.** Greek doctor Diocles promotes the used of peppermint powder for cleaning teeth.

**1543** Andreas Vesalius makes many advances in the study of anatomy and publishes his findings in his famous book, *On the Fabric of the Human Body*.

**1592** Galileo Galilei makes the first thermometer.

**1600s** For almost 30 years, Santorio, an Italian doctor, weighs himself and his food before every meal, and then does the same with his feces, to show that part of the food is extracted by the digestive system.

**1628** Physician and anatomist William Harvey discovers the true nature of the circulation of blood inside the body.

**1660** Robert Hooke builds a compound microscope and discovers body cells

**1714** Daniel Gabriel Fahrenheit devises the Fahrenheit temperature scale, with the zero measure based on the freezing point of sea

water, and the 100 degree mark set at the human body temperature. More accurate measurements showed that a normal body temperature was 98°F (37°C).

**1743** Astronomer Anders Celsius invents the Celsius temperature scale with the 0° and 100° points set at the melting and boiling points of pure water.

**1780** Antoine Lavoisier and Pierre Simon Laplace invent the calorimeter.

**1795** Nicolas Appert develops a new system of preserving food by heating it in sealed containers.

**1816** René Laënnec makes the first stethoscope.

**1831** Scientists in the United States, Germany, and France discover the anesthetic properties of chloroform.

**1842** Surgeon Crawford Long carries out the first pain-free operation using ether as an anesthetic.

**1850s–1880s** Microbiologists Louis Pasteur and Robert Koch discover that microorganisms cause many diseases.

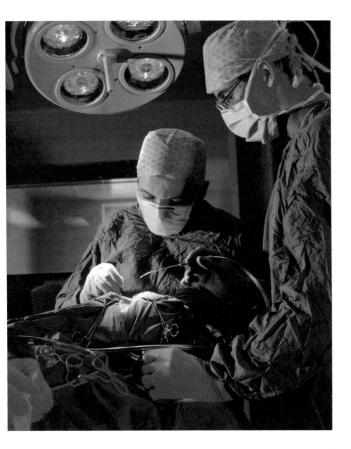

**1930** John H. Gibbon invents a heart-lung machine.

**1952** Physician Robert Lee Wild produces the first ultrasound images of structures inside the body.

**1953** The structure of deoxyribonucleic acid (DNA) is determined by James Watson and Francis Crick.

**1958** Rune Elmqvist makes the first heart pacemaker.

**1967** Surgeon Christiaan Barnard carries out the first human-to-human heart transplant.

**1972** Janet Mertz and Ron Davis use cut-and-paste techniques to make the first recombinant DNA engineered by humans.

**1977** Raymond Damadian takes the first pictures inside the human body using magnetic resonance imaging (MRI).

**1996** Dolly the sheep is the first mammal to be cloned. She dies in 2003, several years earlier than expected, although it is unclear if her death was caused by her cloned DNA.

**2003** The Human Genome Project produces an almost complete library of the chemical sequence of every human gene. However, research continues into what each strand of DNA does.

**1856** Louis Pasteur (left) develops his system of pasteurization, following his discovery that bacteria and other "germs" cause disease.

**1860s** Gregor Mendel studies plant breeding and lays the foundations of genetics.

**1865** Joseph Lister performs the first antiseptic operation.

**1881** Louis Pasteur demonstrates a vaccine against anthrax.

**1910** Salvarsan, the first synthetic chemical cure—discovered by Paul Ehrlich and Sahachiro Hata—begins to be sold.

**1914** A team at Johns Hopkins Hospital in Baltimore makes the first kidney dialysis machine.

**1928** Alexander Fleming discovers penicillin, an antibiotic. The drug becomes widely used in the 1940s.

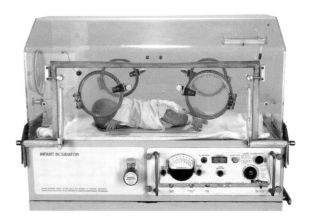

**anatomy** The arrangement of body parts, such as tissues and organs, inside the body of a living organism, and the science of identifying and describing these parts.

**ancient Greece** A civilization that existed on the mainland and islands of modern-day Greece and Turkey between 2000 and 300 B.C.

**anesthetic** A chemical that renders a patient unable to feel pain.

**antibody** A protein produced by the body's immune system in response to foreign substances, or antigens. Many different types of antibodies are made, each able to bind to a particular antigen. Once antibodies have bound, the antigen can be engulfed and destroyed by white blood cells.

**antigen** A protein, toxin, or other large molecule to which the body reacts by producing antibodies.

**bacteria** Single-celled microorganisms that are present almost everywhere on Earth. Bacteria can only be seen through a microscope, and most are spherical, rodlike, or spiral in shape. Some bacteria are beneficial to people, helping us digest our food and playing an important part in the preparation of some foods. Others, however, are responsible for serious diseases such as cholera.

**electromagnetic radiation** Waves made up of electric and magnetic fields. Electromagnetic waves travel at the speed of light, but the characteristics of a particular wave are determined by its frequency. Radio waves and microwaves are low-frequency electromagnetic waves, while infrared, visible light, ultraviolet, and X rays are produced as the frequency increases.

**enzyme** A biological catalyst—a protein molecule produced by an organism to control or perform a particular chemical reaction.

**epidemic** A disease outbreak in which people fall ill more quickly than usual.

**fermentation** The breakdown of sugars to release energy. In certain conditions some types of yeast and other microorganisms release carbon dioxide and alcohol as waste products from fermentation, an effect that is used in breadmaking and brewing.

**genetic** Relating to, or the study of, the inherited features of an organism.

**hormone** A substance released by certain glands into the bloodstream that travels to and acts on remote sites in the body. Both natural hormones and artificial hormones are often used in medicine.

**immunize** To protect from the effects of a harmful substance or disease. There are two forms of immunization—passive, which involves injecting the patient with antibodies, and active, in which a form of harmful substance that has been made harmless in some way is injected, allowing the patient to generate antibodies toward it.

**Industrial Revolution** A great change in social and economic organization brought about by the replacement of hand tools by machines and power tools, and the development of large-scale industrial production methods. The Industrial Revolution started in England around 1760 and spread to the rest of Europe and the United States.

**magnetism** All phenomena associated with magnets and magnetic fields.

Magnetic fields are regions around magnets in which a force acts on any magnet or electric charge present.

**magnets** Any material capable of generating a magnetic field.

**microorganism** An organism too small to be seen with the eye alone. For example, bacteria, viruses, and yeasts.

**microwave** An electromagnetic wave with a wavelength between 1 mm and 300 mm. Microwaves are used for radar, communications, and heating foods.

**plague** A deadly disease that spreads through a population. The Black Death was a disease called bubonic plague, spread by the fleas of rats.

**positrons** Positively charged subatomic particles with the same mass as electrons. Positrons are very unstable and rapidly react with any matter to form gamma rays.

**protons** Basic components of atoms. Protons are located in the nucleus and have a positive electric charge.

**radiation** The act of giving off radioactive particles, heat, or electromagnetic waves.

**radioactivity** The disintegration of atomic nuclei accompanied by the giving off of particles or electromagnetic waves.

**recombinant DNA** DNA molecules that have been created by artificially pasting together DNA fragments that are often taken from different species.

**Rome** The ancient civilization that began in the Italian city of Rome around 700 B.C. and had established a vast empire around the Mediterranean by 200 A.D. The Romans are noted for being the first to bring law and order to Europe and for their great works of engineering. Roman—noun, adjective

**trepanning** A primitive surgical procedure in which a hole is cut in the skull to release pressure.

**vaccine** A medication, often containing disease-causing microorganisms that have been killed or weakened, which is administered to immunize or increase immunity to a particular illness.

**virus** A tiny, disease-causing particle that consists of protein combined with genetic material (DNA or RNA—ribonucleic acid). Viruses are only capable of replicating inside living cells, and for this reason many scientists do not consider them to be living organisms; other scientists, however, consider them to be a type of microorganism.

**white blood cells** Components of the blood responsible for destroying foreign substances and organisms. Different types of white blood cells perform different functions in this process, which is called the immune response. Some generate antibodies, while others engulf and digest foreign particles.

**World War I (1914–1918)** A war fought mainly in Europe between the Central Powers—Germany, the Austro-Hungarian Empire (present-day Austria and Hungary), and the Ottoman Empire (now Turkey)—and the Allies: France, the British Empire, Russia, and the United States. The Allies eventually won the conflict, but millions of soldiers on both sides lost their lives.

**World War II (1939–1945)** The most destructive conflict in history, fought mainly in Europe, East Asia, and North Africa. The Axis powers (Germany, Austria, Japan, and Italy) were opposed by the Allies (Britain, the United States, France, and the USSR). Germany surrendered in April 1945, but Japan fought on until August, when atomic weapons dropped by U.S. aircraft destroyed the Japanese cities of Hiroshima and Nagasaki.

**X ray** A type of electromagnetic radiation with a wavelength between 0.001 and 10 nm. X rays are able to travel through soft tissues and can be used to study the internal structures of the body.

# FURTHER RESOURCES

## Books

*The History of Medicine* by Michael Woods and Mary B. Woods. Minneapolis, MN: Twenty First Century Books, 2006.

*Future Techniques in Surgery* by Sandra and Owen Giddens. New York: Rosen Pub. Group, 2003.

*Joseph Lister and the Story of Antiseptics* by John Bankston. Hockessin, DE: Mitchell Lane Publishers, 2005.

*The Story of Pharmaceuticals: How They Changed the World* by Natalie M. Rosinsky. Mankato, MN: Compass Point Books, 2010.

## Websites

*Science Museum, London: Brought to Life*
http://www.sciencemuseum.org.uk/broughttolife.aspx

*Discovery Channel: Alternative Medicine Cabinet*
http://health.discovery.com/centers/althealth/cabinet/cabinet.html

*EdHeads: Virtual Knee Surgery*
http://www.edheads.org/activities/knee

*School Science: History of Medicine*
http://resources.schoolscience.co.uk/abpi/history/index.html

# INDEX

## A

acetominophen 29
amputation 10, 12–13
analgesics 31
anatomy 7–8, 10
ancient Egyptians 4–7, 11, 24
anesthesia 13–15, 31, 40, 51
animal testing 30
anthrax 16, 18, 20
antibiotics 26–28, 31
antibodies 21, 42
antigens 41
antiseptic 10, 19
Asclepius. Greek god of healing 4
aspirin 6, 22, 28–31

## B

bacteriology 15–15, 18, 26, 27
Black Death 7
blood 6–9, 11, 14, 21, 23, 25–6, 28, 30–33, 35, 38–46, 48, 51, 59
blood circulation 9
blood pressure 35
blood types 41–42

## C

caesarian section 52
caffeine 22
cancer 12, 28, 30–31, 58
Chain, Ernst 27
chloroform 14–15
cholera 16, 20
chromosomes 53, 58
circumcision 50
cloning 59
computed tomography 37
contraceptives 24, 54–55
cowpox 17
cyclosporin 41

## D

Davy, Humphry 13, 15
diagnosis 6, 32–36, 38
dialysis machine 42–43
DNA 53, 57–58
drugs 6, 22–26, 28–31, 41, 46, 51, 57

## E

Ehrlich, Paul 22
electrocardiograph 34
electroencephalograms 34

endoscope 35, 48
epidemics 7, 20
ether 14, 15

## F–G

Fleming, Alexander 26
Florey, Howard 27
Freud, Sigmund 13
Galen 8–10
genes 53, 58–59
germ theory 15
Greek medicine 4–5, 7, 24, 32–33, 36, 50

## H

Harvey, William 8–9, 41
hearing aids 47
heart 6, 8, 9, 28, 34, 36, 42–46, 48, 58
heart-lung machine 43–44
herbal remedies 5, 6, 8, 10, 32, 24
Hippocrates 6–7
hospitals 8, 12–13, 15, 19, 38
hygiene 7, 50–51

## I

ibuprofen 29, 31
immunosuppressant drugs 41
Indian medicine 23, 33
infant incubator 54
infection 10, 12, 19, 27–29, 31
IVF 56–57

## J–M

Jenner, Edward 17
Koch, Robert 15–16, 18, 32
laughing gas 13, 15
leprosy 10, 18, 29
Lister, Joseph 19
liver 9, 25
Long, Crawford 15
magnetic resonance imaging 38–39
malaria 18, 23, 25
medical schools 8
mental illness 13, 26, 38
microorganisms 14–16, 28, 32–33, 51
microscope 6, 16, 32
midwives 50–51
mosquito 7, 23, 25

## N–Q

Nightingale, Florence 13
nursing 13

pacemaker 45–46
Pasteur, Louis 15–16, 20, 32, 51
pasteurization 16
penicillin 22, 24, 26, 28
petri dishes 18
pharmacy 31
plague 7, 10, 17–18
*Plasmodium* 25
plastic surgery 41, 49
pneumonia 24
positron emission tomography 38
prehistoric medicine 4–5
psychiatry 13
psychoanalysis 13
public baths 7
quinine 23

## R

rabies 18
robotic surgery 49
Roman medicine 5, 7–8, 10–11, 32
Röntgen, Wilhelm 36
Rorschach, Hermann 13

## S

sedatives 31
silicone implant 46
smallpox 17–18
stethoscope 36, 51
supernatural medicine 4, 6
surgery 10–11, 19, 26,31, 35, 40–46, 48–49, 52
symptoms 6, 22, 34
syphilis 10, 18, 24
syringe 12, 14

## T

temperature 6, 20, 34–35, 44
thermometer 6, 34–35
tranquilizers 31
transfusion 41–42
trepanning 4–5
tuberculosis 16, 24
twins 41, 58

## U–X

ultrasound 36–37, 52, 57
vaccine 17–18, 20–21
Van Leeuwenhoek, Anton 16
Vesalius, Andreas 8
X rays 36–38